BE SURPRISED
Own Your Courage and Self Trust

Paul Fashade B.SC, M.A.

AuthorHouse™ *UK Ltd.*
500 Avebury Boulevard
Central Milton Keynes, MK9 2BE
www.authorhouse.co.uk
Phone: 08001974150

© 2010 Paul Fashade B.SC, M.A.. All rights reserved.

No part of this book may be reproduced, stored in a retrieval system, or transmitted by any means without the written permission of the author.

First published by AuthorHouse   11/11/2010

ISBN: 978-1-4490-9276-4 (sc)
ISBN: 978-1-4490-9275-7 (hc)

This book is printed on acid-free paper.

CONTENTS

Chapter 1. A crucial beginning… 1
Chapter 2. What exactly are we surviving for? 11
Chapter 3. Your Intelligent Thinking Heart! 23
Chapter 4. The joy of worrying…! 51
Chapter 5. Crucial ways to get back if you think you have no time! 59
Chapter 6. Heart-fully, Happy and Content Now, Regardless! 85
Chapter 7. The big "Why" tale…and even more inspiring questions… 99
Chapter 8. The Main Key "ki" To Open Our Senses… 107
Chapter 9. Looking At Your Life. Can You Call It a Blessing? 117
Chapter 10. Open Intelligence, The Ultimate Wisdom To All Truths…that opens our thinking heart…...121
Chapter 11. The Best Gift… 137
Chapter 12. Building a Backbone, Not a Wishbone! 143
Chapter 13. Finally Letting Go of Our Past 153
Chapter 14. How To Access Yourself When Lost! 159
Chapter 15. The Final Analysis – My Constant Reminder! .167
Chapter 16. Inspiring Stories and Clear Insights! 179
Chapter 17. More Actions To Bring You Back To Yourself Quickly… 205
Chapter 18. Choose Genuine or False being. The price…......215

CHAPTER 1

A CRUCIAL BEGINNING...

*The world is truly heaven and then we
create our own hell through fear!*

If you question anything doubtfully enough, eventually you will doubt it. It is inevitable. And then we wonder why we doubt most things and often ourselves. Moreover, we never get where we dream to go. Always look for what is left unsaid in any news, as these gaps are where the truth really exists, not the version you are supposed to hear, or your fearful head spins on. Years of working for the Ministry Of Defence made this very clear for me and it shows how our thinking is mirrored (and even distorted) by our mind but the genuine truth can only be found in our inner guide.

"Be you; everybody else is already taken."
Oscar Wilde

"Imagine you are working on a jigsaw puzzle. You put pieces together in one corner and you can see a small house. You may work on a completely

different area next and a tree might appear. They don't seem to be connected until later, when you work on another part and a country scene unfolds. The tree and the house are complete within themselves, but they are also parts of the bigger picture. You may have already discovered that seemingly unimportant things you learned, jobs you took and experiences you had, all fit together in a way you couldn't have anticipated at the time. It was only later, when you saw the bigger picture, that you realized the importance of certain things. Your higher self has a larger plan for your life and every experience you have will fit together and give you value in some way, even if you don't yet know."
Sanaya Roman

We can never truly know the future, we can only fool ourselves into thinking we know. It's an illusion created from mind analysis, judgements and expectations in our own bubble, while nature, the world and the universe does what it does best - to keep surprising us. It's never personal even if we think so! Therefore, we must "plan to be surprise" so we do not fear what our future holds.

> **To make life easier and clear, we must begin making it a must to "plan to be surprised". This means to practise and live with more acceptance regardless of what we think, so that fear has less charge on us for what is to come, as we can never truly know the future.**

I feel I need to share something rather important about my surprise at writing this book. Firstly, I was tagged dyslexic very late at 18 and with an attention deficit disorder and told in short that I may not amount to much due to my slow ability to read and write. I had however, the ability to learn and remember most things I heard and saw with relative ease. I used this skill for my exams as far back as I can remember but still I hated reading and writing. So I kept reading to a minimum for my university exams preferring to listen and discuss things with my lecturers. If you do not fit into the required boxes of how you should read, write, interact and pass exams, you are considered stupid or tagged somehow deficient, limited or lacking, when all it actually means is that usually you have other gifts or skills unexplored with a different way at getting to the same place or one's true path.

I never thought I would ever write a book, but here I am and I also never thought I would study beyond university but here I am. The funny thing is that I have always felt I would write even when I was young and labelled very differently. So I say never fully buy into however any "experts" tag you! Hear it and use it as a guide, then do what your heart says with the gifts or skills you know deep down. Trust yourself to do things your own way heart-fully, without ego, as you will only pleasantly surprise yourself, and others will benefit by default, whether you mean to or not. That is the beauty about having the courage to stay with and live your truth.

The best surprise is when you truly get beyond your over thinking and when you step into the real you without blame, judgement or analysis. I am certain that you will be very surprised with the things that come thereafter and they will "wow" you.

"Whatever you can do or dream you can, begin it. Boldness has genius, magic, and power in it. Begin it now." GOETHE

One boy's choice for life…

On a much more personal note, here is a story of the shaping of a little boy's life and true path that I would like to share with you. This boy loved and adored his parents no matter what they said or did to him. At the age of six he started wetting his bed with no knowledge of the reason why. Wetting his bed was always followed by pain. Pain caused by being beaten with whips or sticks by his parents in the belief that this punishment would help him stop this bad habit. The boy did not complain or feel that he did not deserve the whips as he loved his parents and thought for certain they did their best to help him.

He soon realised to avoid future pain he needed to adapt. So every night when he realised his bed was wet he would get up quietly, pull his bed out onto the balcony, and wait several hours for it to dry, as they lived in a warm climate. He would then drag the bed back and cover it up with newspaper so the remaining stain would not show. He slept away from the spot cramped on the corner of the bed so it would dry. The boy also had to make sure he washed the stain off the bed sheets to ensure they were dry before he went to bed the next night. This daily ritual went on for many years until he was about 13 years old. Some days he would not have the luxury of time so he would have to adapt and just use lots of dry paper to absorb the wetness.

When he missed something or forgot to get up and was discovered he would take the beating. He would accept it because it was his fault for not getting up on time; and he would take it without crying too much. His parents believed this punishment was working as most days he would not wet his bed or so they thought. The boy would feel good and confident, as he was smart enough to adapt and not be found out which gave him more courage to adapt some more, so all would go well. He continued to love, respect and obey his parents regardless.

At the age of 13, on a beautiful summer's day, he went to a community club where he met his friends who were all on a summer break. There he had one of the best days of his life, swimming, laughing and much more, as kids do. This day was particularly special as he made two new friends for the first time and he ended up coming home late and was so tired that he went to bed early. He did not wake up until around 5 am when he noticed to his horror that his bed was soaking wet, worse than ever before. In a panic, he dragged the bed to the balcony and washed the bed sheets. The boy was still feeling very tired from his day's activities and while the sheets and bed were drying out on the balcony he went into the bathroom and curled up on the end part of the bathtub on the cold tiles. He laid down and quickly fell asleep leaving the lights on so he would not sleep for too long.

His mum saw the lights when she woke up in the morning. The next thing the boy realised was the door of the bathroom swung open to find he was discovered by his mum. She looked at him with shock and surprise, finally realising what had actually been going on for years. He had never seen such an expression on her face in his entire life. She quietly asked him to go and wash himself then sleep in her room. At this point, the boy was terrified of the punishment to come and so he remained wide-awake. He was waiting in his mother's room as surely his father would find out, and all hell would break loose.

He waited and waited but nothing happened and when his mother came in, she looked at him surprised and yet with kind eyes. She did not say much but made sure the boy was fine. He felt loved, like he had always believed and he slept most of the day and did not go to school. His parents replaced the mattress with a new one and never beat him about the bed wetting anymore.

And about 6 weeks later this boy stopped wetting his bed.

This little boy learnt to accept, not blame, nor judge or analyse what was wrong. He just stayed with the situation and adapted. He took the consequences of what happened if he did not adapt. Little did he know how well this would serve him in later life.

As you may have guessed, I was this little boy. This experience inspired me to do things that may seem impossible at first, even if it felt like the pain would never end. **I never give too much credit to my thoughts that don't help me much.** I have learnt to work with my mind ever since. I began to really understand how mind framing works. I began to see a cycle of constant slides backwards, excessive self doubt, the "ifs", "shoulds", or "maybes". If one wants to genuinely access oneself, one must practice lightening the mind load and then accepting the situation in that particular moment. I just wanted to share my start with you. Therefore, you too can realise that you can work with your mind at anytime in your life and that it will make a rooted difference to your quality of life, no matter the heaviness or clouds around you. I never saw this experience as a bad thing. I took responsibility for my actions, perhaps at too young an age, but my thoughts were not of hatred or feeling sorry for myself despite being afraid of the painful moments.

I only realised it was not ok when I was an adult and experts tagged the beatings as abuse. However, I never bought into this fully, even when I had put it all to rest within myself, by later in life openly talking about it and making peace with my parents. This shaped me and allowed me to be at ease and fully understand myself for the better and be where I am today with an open heart.

In addition, I had other, even more awakening experiences that occurred later in life and so **I now realise that growth is always continuous and one cannot always hang on to the heavy past. Otherwise, one is buried with it while still alive. If it does not help your life then what makes you do it? And what do you feel will make you stop doing it? It is important to practice living without hate, blame, judgements, nor excessive analysis. Practice complete forgiveness so one can get on with life, the one we are meant to live, as soon as possible, before one's life is fully spent!**

A magical night with a group of stars…

I am standing outside in the Austrian mountains in Flattach, Corinthia and I realise that I am looking at the most beautiful sight I have ever seen at night. The crispest clarity that I have ever witnessed where everything is peaceful and silent and I see mountains covered with lush greenery. As the darkness sets in there is a dusty haze and I can just make out a picturesque view that I can't even use words to describe. I stand here right now observing, watching the light fade and another hour later it shifts into complete darkness. Who I am is completely lit up by the stars above me, billions of them like I have never seen before in my entire life. It is amazing how stars always look so different, wherever you look at them and yet at the same time they look the same, while being dispersed so beautifully and wildly across the sky. You do not know where to start looking and where to finish!

We are all connected at the core with love and care. It links us all together and helps us shine more even if we do not know it most of the time. Just like the stars are dispersed with gaps in between them, small, large, some brighter, some not so bright, but they are all shining above in the same sky.

My heart is very full and overwhelmed in this moment. It has made me realise something crucially important: Why I am genuinely writing this book? Some of the simple clear reasons I wanted to write this book were to share this gift and share the practise 'of the doing'. And to make clear the courage that one must experience which will lead to self-trust and to boldly wake up one's personal genuine power, without one's ego and fear being in the way.

This makes it very easy for me to spontaneously do my heart's will, with determination but always with love for others, even if it's tough love that isn't always nice to hear. I find it best to always speak my truth, not just from my head's thinking, but also from my genuine self that has more freedom and clarity within it.

I am writing this book because I have realised one more thing - happiness is only real when it is shared with others.

We are not meant to be "our own island". Our connection with others satisfies our longing for love and acceptance. We always want to share the incredible things in life with others: sometimes it is just a moment, a look, a smile, and other times it is so much more. Happiness glows in us even more when we share it, it doesn't have to be shared with a loved one… picture the Olympics Gold medallists who have stepped into their true glorious selves and are now celebrating and connecting not only with the whole stadium but all those watching across the world. It just has to be a common interest that lights us all up, automatically getting us all inspired so we forget our head's worrying thoughts and thinking for a short while.

This book is not about telling you what to do, nor ramming spiritual ideas or practical ways that have worked for me down your throat. This book is about guiding and reminding us how to access ourselves, with far less fuss, as we are truly our own experts.

We have just forgotten how to plug into our natural inner guide with ease, as we interfere with ourselves constantly with excessive limiting worrying thoughts. We are carried away mindlessly for far too long, which means slowly edging our true self out, losing ourselves along the way, repeatedly. This book is about coming home to the very genuine you and to finally own and be at ease with your self-trust, courage and thoughts. Instead of looking for your home or where you belong outside yourself, you need to go home first to find your natural secrets, your hidden genuine power already waiting for you!

We like to own many things but we will never truly own ourselves if we do not get clear on who we are. We give up on our life and our spirit so quickly and we hand it over to others so easily. In the end, our things and our toys will come and go…but what about who we are? Ironically, we do not really own anything. We are just caretakers until we pass it on or lose it. After all, we can't take anything with us when we die! The reason you should write a will is to enable you to have a say on who gets the things we treasure once we are dead. If we do not, the taxman will end up speaking for you and deciding who get what, if anything at all!

The only two things that you really need to 'own' are your courage and self-trust as these open the gates to everything else. What I mean is how can you truly love anything or anyone without first trusting yourself? How can you be at your best without self-trust and courage, which will fire up your desire to do things boldly and will shift your fears aside? Self-trust, and courage can only happen if one is genuinely ready to access one's self instead of merely looking or listening to the confusing **"mind led stranger"** that we allow to take charge of us most of our lives.

The question is, do we want to be led by this stranger most of our lives, and have huge regrets when it is too damn late? On the other hand, do we want to trust and lead ourselves to where we genuinely and boldly want to be?

Wrapped around all this are the three words that always change our state into one of fear, worry, and non-resourcefulness. These three words are BLAME, ANALYSIS, and JUDGEMENT. Each of these words rarely helps us, nor kick us into productive actions generated from love and not from destructiveness. Instead, they give rise to hate, jealousy, contempt, anger, irritation, and much worse! These words suck our energy as these words are always charged with unhelpful emotions that lead us away from our genuine true self but instead bring us closer to the "mind led stranger" within us. These words and the thoughts that come from them make both our mind and our true selves constantly lost!

Deep down we dislike this confusing stranger in us that causes such unsettling thoughts and destructive behaviour. Therefore, we trust ourselves far less particularly when we are in doubt and all too often when we are lost in these unhelpful thoughts!

These three words (Blame, Judgement and Analysis) are the nucleus of the web that takes charge of us. When they are no longer the focus, the web's strength and energy simply gets weak and will definitely be blown away. This means that the only thing left will be the genuine truth, awareness and the ability to observe one's own unique and special mind.

Once you live in self-trust and with courage things simply come to you with ease. Life opens itself up to you and you manifest or make things happen just like that. Problems will become just challenges that also fade away with time and people will want to do things with you and will naturally be drawn to you. Life will open up and things will just start happening for you because you finally allow it.

CHAPTER 2

WHAT EXACTLY ARE WE SURVIVING FOR?

What is the missing link to all our actions? Is it just to survive or feel good? Why do we compromise and downplay our lives?

Do we just hold on to our things, create a family, see the world, or is there more inside all of us? Is there another level of our being? Do we feel the connection to all things or do we feel separated?

Why do we sell ourselves short leaving us feeling unfulfilled and a shadow of our true selves? Why do we allow opportunities to slip by while others have the trust and courage to manifest or create their dreams?

It was not that long ago that people were hung or killed for having creative ideas that were anti establishment, religion, or government. Anything outside of those strict confines was considered wrong and/or 'evil' and one would suffer harsh or even fatal consequences.

Fortunately today, if one does not follow the norms in society, **one may be labelled strange or different, but at least you are free to express your genuine spirit! Your own genuine self is the best gift to the world. This gift lies in one's truth, led by your self-trust and self-courage. This important realisation of self-truth and courage will shift the focus from capital gains, which is mostly about money and materials towards social human profit, growth, and opportunities.** Remember that the more people you serve, the greater the abundance and wealth you will gain whether as an individual or an organisation. Genuinely serving others increases your natural wealth. This includes financial growth and will increase if you believe that money also needs to work for you while serving others. You also need to lose your 'lack mentality' by which I mean being obsessed by what you don't have and with what you lack rather than focusing on, being grateful for and, most importantly, enjoying what you do have.

A constant 'lack mentality' will lead you to get lost, lack self-awareness, and kill your true trust and genuine courage. So always be alert and do not be tricked by your mind. If you feel that you are lacking something, it is only in your mind and rarely true.

In order to finally understand and feel it, our search for the truth must begin within us. When your body mind and spirit accepts a truth it will resonate throughout your body and you will vibrate this feeling out to everyone around you. Governments and many organisations pretend they know what is going on in times of uncertainty and change and yet we all know that they are at a loss deep down like most of us. Truth can only come from one's genuine self! We all have our own truth to live by.

To experience this is vital and it is crucial to start this experience immediately. It carries on from us to others, even by default, like a drop of rain that joins in with the power of the river; like a collective heartfelt rhythm beating in one purposeful direction for everyone's benefit and uniquely touching others. Our history is only the history of our collective thoughts. Eventually, we will understand that the sincere truth has always been waiting for us within our hearts. Sometimes truth has a large price tag and most of the time it calls for action to take place now, which will lead to genuine growth. Think how quickly the world's collective thoughts have changed from believing the world to be flat, to abolishing the slave trade, and a start to environmental awareness. The world's thinking is constantly changing and evolving – what truth do we need to discover next?

It is important to be aware that thinking evolved not from thinking alone per se, but from what we have experienced previously. This includes things that we were not ready to have a closer look at the time and so quickly forgot. Fortunately, some individuals managed to step into their genuine truth and as a result could not hold back a new discovery or development any longer. We all continue to benefit from those individuals who acted on their desire, courage, and self-truth.

We all have this calling deep down for what is true for us and what must be done. Knowing why is irrelevant, that is just our stranger's thinking, slowing us down, and trying to prevent us. The real reasons usually show up later and can't always be known at the start. With or without goals our joy must always be in the experience of doing it heart-fully, with courage and self-truth. What else are we waiting for? What are we surviving for and to what benefit exactly? I can verify this in my own life now and in my past. The rewards and effects on my own well being from self-growth are both amazing and immense. When individuals act on their own truth, trusting themselves completely, despite all odds against them, they then easily have the courage to connect with their own heart and spirit to create amazing things.

It is important to know that our body and mind rarely deliver without our complete self-trust and courage coming from our hearts. Self-belief, without doubt, naturally flows from the heart. It has led individuals to become aware of our beautiful planet and to understand that if they heart-fully choose from their deepest guide then they can create whatever they perceive possible. These are not just words, the evidence is around us daily from amazing inventions to other beautiful creations, and from ordinary individuals to the ones we call great.

These individuals are no different from us. They just learnt to access themselves better, trusted themselves more, and most definitely acted courageously on it. That is it! Courage and self-truth will take us to a new stage of evolution where we will truly rise up, away from our past self possessed thoughts or illusions. Only when we reach into our hearts and ask our genuine guide about what stands true for us can we lighten our fear-led thoughts and step up to do what we previously deemed impossible. Only when our hearts answer the question 'what if' does our clarity flow from there and many amazing things are created for the greater good of us all. In brutal contrast, the "me only" approach, with the ego fully charged, usually leads to separation with no self-trust, nor for others, including self-doubt, self-sabotage and worse the destruction of our society!

We learn and grow from our heart's truth, which sometimes requires pain and suffering, in order to gain insight, inspiration and clarity but which will eventually set us free.

This rarely comes from thinking. If you do a quick flash back and observe your history it does not usually make logical sense, but only makes full sense when we are more engaged with our natural intelligent senses (getting conscious). When we get conscious with ourselves, our higher state of energy creates clarity and determination and in this state of enthusiasm, we can do almost anything.

We have all been in this conscious state, that feeling of flow, even if it has only been for a moment. It is a wonderful feeling we need to plug into more frequently rather than merely getting there by accident or by fluke! What does it mean to you to be consciously aware? Is that important for your daily life? How can you plug into this state easily and often? To become consciously aware is easy and natural - we just need to go within and begin to breathe deeply. Be in the silence. Be still long enough to feel yourself in your moments. This will shift you towards peace and tranquillity within your body; the answers you seek will then come to you with ease.

How to stop beating your self up with unhelpful thoughts!

In order to create the space for love in your life one's heart needs to be open to give and receive love. This is not always easy. One needs to embrace forgiveness, kindness, patience, and trust. Love does not magnify by itself.

> **Embrace forgiveness in your heart, embrace forgiveness for your self, embrace forgiveness of others and embrace forgiveness and release your past pain. Stop beating yourself up and stop trying to carry those past experiences around with you like a dead weight; then you will no longer feel heavy, sad, and uncomfortable but journey unburdened to new places and new experiences, feeling lighter.**

When I decided to forgive others and importantly myself, my heart was relieved from some sort of self-imposed prison. I was able to be at ease, sleep without the aid of pills or remedies, and I was able to feel genuine love and care again. It is truly that simple.

Forgiveness needs to be a daily practice, so the negative loads can't root themselves, hurting us and making us a stranger to ourselves.

I truly know that the key to genuine happiness is to be fully stimulated by courage and self-trust. These are simply the chillies that fire up your soul to rise above all pettiness and mind-drama distractions and allow us to do great things beyond those we previously believed impossible!!

It is always excessive thinking that slows everything down or stops us dead in our tracks of self-truth. I simply do what my heart wills and everything else falls into place. I take in a new experience knowing what is possible for me in that moment. Little by little I gain ground and my thoughts control me less as my heartfelt actions lead me to my truth. I then access my inner guide more clearly. I increasingly trust myself and the more I do my heart's will the better I feel. I know that I have everything in me that I need to do things… now, not later!

To love one must learn to forgive - period! Forgiveness is the key to courage; self- trust and then the rest will open itself to you.

Your energy will rise and be on your side. When we have unhelpful thoughts, we literally feel our energy leaving us, shrinking us away. We are exhausted, frustrated, and fed up and we will age much faster! It is a slow kill. We all feel the suffering in our bodies so how do we stop this mad mind-drama, heal our deep pain and live again? We do not need to stop our thoughts, we simply need to listen to our hearts more and observe our thinking without blame and judgement. This will stop us from reacting so that we can genuinely respond, instead.

"Those who cannot change their minds cannot change anything."
George Bernard Shaw

When we get a grip and become aware of our restless unhelpful thoughts and behaviours then we will completely wake up, as we will have learnt our truth by ourselves without all the doubts. **Our natural courage comes from our heart and when our roots are firmly grounded. We grow our own tree from those strong roots and then we can share our truth and joy with others like a tree that bears fruit.**

Our strength and our growth will simply inspire others to do the same and, if that is not enough reason for you, then just do it for you. People will automatically benefit from you doing your heart's will by default. You just need to look at our history and the amazing things we have created. We see that other individuals through finding their courage and backbone, including following their heartfelt truth has allowed them to do their magic, which has also led to creativity beyond logical thinking.

I speak from my own personal experience as well as from studies, research, and breakthroughs with clients and seen and felt miracles in both my life and others. I have travelled around the world observing different cultures, working with individuals in the Army, Navy, Royal Air Force, and have been coaching and training people for many years. All these experiences have something in common; they have clearly shown me the courageous power of the human spirit. Forgive yourself and your past history, especially for the things you did wrong or whatever you hang on to… you won't die if you let it go…if anything, it will set you free! I have seen this transform many people's lives as well as my own.

We think and say that it is others that are wrong and that they have done this to us but have they and does it really matter now? Especially where you now are in your life? What difference does it make hanging onto those thoughts? Has it made things better? Do you feel good from it?

We are the only ones in our prison. We are responsible for locking ourselves in! Other people do not decide what clothes we wear today, what food we eat, when we brush our teeth, what shampoo or hair products we do not buy, nor where we must live. All these decisions we make ourselves. No other person has the power to make your decisions unless you allow them to. As soon as you realise your own power and not give it to someone else, you will be able to do what comes naturally to you.

We hold onto things in our heads that do not always help us. They were only designed to make us learn so we can grow and live some more. However, we hold onto such thoughts and things as if they mean everything to us, yet they are nothing. They are worth nothing! They are like the waste we put into the toilet. It's just memories brought to life and made real by our lack of forgiveness for others and for ourselves, which leads us to fear even more!

The moment when things do change for the better is when we simply, and consciously, flush them. We do not retrieve our waste and analyse it do we! My raw analogy is intended for its directness and not to offend. Put simply, one has a choice if one wants to feel better…

Our body uses what it can and disposes of what it cannot use. When it overloads we see our body deform, age faster, slowly changing shape, and we start to feel run down too often. Our body cannot clean itself fast enough for us to reload more 'stuff' that does not nourish nor help us. Even when we abuse our body physically, emotionally, and spiritually, our body still tries its best to keep us well, alive and healthy until it just simply can't anymore. We know and feel it long before our body succumbs to our bad habits. Our body then forces us to get well, such as stopping us eating more non-nourishing foods and staying in bed to recover! However we turn on ourselves too often and ignore the problems we create. Over a long period, our body breaks down on us and we may become more seriously ill. Where is the joy or fun in that? We have the power to change our thoughts to create better habits so we can regenerate, making our bodies well again and stay well for longer.

Charged thoughts and their weight!

The funny thing is we can't even see our unhelpful thoughts, unlike the 'stuff' we fill up with and call food or nourishment. We can't even touch nor smell them. They are just a memory strand that has been given so much charge, and so much weight that it is killing us. They can kill us slowly and/or quite quickly depending on how much charge, we give those unhelpful thoughts. Worse still, we get lost in our heads for so long. It is like sleep walking through life. You have a choice to add fuel to your unhelpful thoughts and increase their fire or you can diffuse them by extinguishing out the fire or losing the excess load!

It does not matter if we die today or if we die tomorrow, we are, in effect, already dead because we are not present here anymore. We are stuck in the past or somewhere in limbo. **It is only our 'mind-led stranger' that is present and we feel it and know it hence, we are miserable. No matter what we do to try and escape, we always find this stranger repeatedly. Yet we know it is not our true self. To say no to the stranger we must gain courage and self-trust.**

It is important to observe the shadow in us and it should be done without judgement, blame, or analysis. Once we can see how our shadow or how our illusions are created and/or fed, we have a better handle on making other choices that are more helpful and more in harmony with our true self.

This is the purpose, the start of living our lives, a life without constant slippage and self-doubt. We are our own experts and we are our own guides. It is in all of us and it is only revealed when we are ready. In this book, you will uncover a process that will bring you closer to yourself effortlessly and naturally. I promise that even you will be shocked by how easy the work or practise to get your own courage and self-trust is and it is from courage and self-trust that everything else will grow!

An important story about two dogs…

One dog was a disciplined intelligent dog, he went to dog school, higher education, college, and university while the other dog was a happy street dog. One day out in the real world, the disciplined dog kept running around trying to catch his tail as dogs do. Along came the street dog and saw him running around in circles so he came nearer to observe him more closely.

The street dog asked, "What are you doing?"

The disciplined intelligent dog replied: "Chasing my tail, nothing new, and it's very normal in the dog world. Don't you know that when you finally catch it, this is what makes us extremely happy?"

"What do you mean?" said the street dog.

He replied: "In all my learning from school, my parents, higher education, and dog university, I have been told that if you can catch your tail and stay with it as long as possible you will be happy. The norm is that happiness is in our tail behind or in front of us, depending on which way we are told or led to spin."

The street dog replied: "Hmm, I wasn't aware of that. I have always gone about doing things by creating or feeling my way through even when I am not sure which path I should take. If I wanted to eat, I would eat. If I wanted to catch something, I would catch it. If I wanted to do something, I would just do it, with far less thinking. I just simply seek out what heart-fully feels good and true to me at the time. I find by doing this my tail just follows me around wherever I go. Despite many challenges, I am effortlessly happy in my own experiences. I never had as much learning, schooling, university, teaching and training as you have had, but I guess I was also guided somehow."

Most things we learn in life and study are all guides. They are not set in concrete but many of us blindly follow them to the letter. However, we need to be guided by what feels genuinely true to us, be our own reference resource, acknowledge our real internal voice that is like a light switch just waiting to be turned on. It is there to help us so we can decide what resonates or feels true to us. When we use our inner guide or heartfelt truth, we breathe deeply and decide more quickly and with greater ease. We can then take action without our mind spinning and forever debating with ourselves what is right or wrong!

We need to trust ourselves, our heartfelt truth will always speak to us if we ask or just simply plug into our inner guide. It just needs genuine practise.

However at the start your ego will try and do the talking so don't confuse what you feel with what your ego is trying to make you believe. A simple way of recognising this is if your body feels in conflict with the guidance you have just received from within. In other words, if you feel any discomfort in your stomach or gut then it means your body disagrees. It's time ask yourself questions to properly check it.

What could be even worse is that you may find that you have spent so much time in your mind that you do not even feel your body and don't hear your body talking, even screaming at you trying to let you know that it's time to stop. When this occurs, then seek out someone or something that can shift you back to your true genuine self, as this distress to your body will make your true self a shadow of who you really are! Things rarely get better from this point onwards!

You can learn how to get clarity by the simple power of asking the right questions that will help you plug into your truth. When we accept this truth inside of us, our heads will then follow and this will lead us into action because it resonates brightly with us.

If we are struggling to trust our inner guide, or heartfelt truth, we simply need to strengthen our self-awareness muscle. When we ask heartfelt questions, we do not judge, blame or analyse our response. It is a bit like going to the gym, the muscle you work on the most gets the most developed. You will get more of whatever you focus on or wherever your thoughtful mind spends most of its time. Remember this.

A Deluded Day and Nightmare of the Past!

Does our past have a hold on us? Do we manipulate situations and people to get what we want? Of course we do! Our past fears and our 'lack mentality' make us behave in this way. It is a false sense of security. We use our stories to gain sympathy or use sarcasm to show ourselves as a victim all the time trying to manipulate

people into giving us love or something; it is control through the back door!

It is such a demeaning way of connecting. It makes us even more of a shadow of our true self. We are, in effect, victimising ourselves, making ourselves so small, just in the hope that other people will like us or love us. Once this victimisation has been discovered, the other person begins to feel drained of his or her own good, natural energy. One will become more isolated and alone, resentful, bitter and what he or she fears the most may come to fruition. What one thinks about, one brings about.

R.I.P. – The past you can never change!

Most of your past history won't help you now so this is the death of your old life and you now have a new life, a rebirth. Imagine if you did not have to live up to your own past history, your old image or old reputation, who do you feel you could become? How do you honestly feel you would live your life? What decisions do you feel you would make differently?

When we share our happiness, we connect with the living again. Life starts to happen for us more easily. It is like you are now more openly awake and the universe (or your God) is now there to give you your gifts that have always been waiting for you.

When you surrender and let go of your past, you make room for infinite possibilities.

If you have understood what you are supposed to learn from your past situation or the old you then bury your coffin with your good old self in there. Purposefully bury your coffin, put some soil over it, write the epitaph for the old you, but at the end of the night, when you have been there all day, walk away from the grave into the land of the living and be born again. Why not? If you can't physically bury it just leave it in the cemetery with the other graves but make sure you walk away from it anyway.

CHAPTER 3

YOUR INTELLIGENT THINKING HEART!

Your Thinking Heart

Can your heart think and store memories?

A number of years ago, Claire Silvia from Boston , USA , had a heart transplant. Pretty soon, she started to experience strange things. "It was like a whole new rhythm, a whole new feeling," she explains. And when a journalist asked her, soon after the transplant, what she now wanted most in the world, the words "I'd die for a beer right now!" suddenly popped out of her mouth, much to her embarrassment and surprise – she didn't previously even like beer! "Little by little," she says, "other things started happening until I was convinced I was living with the presence of another within me." Claire not only noticed changes in her tastes, her preferences for foods and drinks, but also even in her handwriting. All she knew of the person who had donated her heart was that he was a young man who died in a motorcycle accident, strict confidentiality rules mean that organ recipients aren't allowed to know the details of their donor. Then one night she dreamed of her donor, and the name 'Tim L' popped into her mind.

The next day she rang her transplant co-ordinator and told her about the changes she had experienced, and asked her if her donor's name was in fact Tim L. There was silence on the other end of the phone, and then the co-ordinator said, "Please don't pursue this".

It turned out that her donor's name was in fact Tim Lamarand.

Throughout most of Human history, people didn't locate their thoughts and emotions within the brain. For example, the ancient Egyptians didn't even see fit to preserve the brains of their kings and queens in the same way that they did with other organs when mummifying them. But while it wasn't until recently that the brain was identified as the seat of our thoughts, emotions, or soul, then where did the ancients believe was the centre of these things? The answer is the heart.

Today we laugh at the notion that our hearts could be intelligent, we see them as basic pumps. A pump doesn't have thoughts, emotions and memories. But perhaps we don't know as much as we think we do. For example, our modern association of thought and emotion with the brain may have gone a bit too far.

One association with the heart that we have still kept, to some extent, is that it's something to do with our emotions, particularly with love – the heart remains a popular visual symbol of love. Also it's often used as a symbol for our intuition and morals. We often use phrases like "listen to your heart". Or "follow what your heart tells you is right". Admittedly, most people when using these phrases are not always literally asking you to stop and try to sense how your heart feels, they are using the word 'heart' as a metaphor for your intuition. But could that metaphor for locating feelings and emotions in the heart actually have some reality to it?

Well, at the most basic level, we know that emotional stress can harm the health of our heart, putting them under strain, and perhaps leading – in extreme cases – to people suffering heart attacks, as the end product of years of chronic stress. Also, the heart regulates the blood flow, and blood contains hormones and neuro-peptides which transmit emotional information. But could there be a stronger connection than this?

Amazingly, Dr Andrew Armour, a neurologist from Montreal , Canada , discovered a small but complex network of neurons in the heart, which he has dubbed 'the little brain in the heart'. These neurons seem to be capable of both short and long term memory. Why should the heart even have neurons and the ability to remember? Well, for one thing, there is a lot of muscle co-ordination that goes on in the heart in order to allow it to function properly. The fact that hearts can even be transplanted shows that there is a long-term memory stored in the heart for its rhythms. When a heart is removed, it is cooled and can stay alive for up to four hours. Once the heart is connected into its new recipient, as blood enters it, it begins to beat again. It is almost certainly the 'little brain in the heart' that is enabling the heart to remember how to beat.

Furthermore, there is a lot of communication that occurs between the heart and the brain. There are 40,000 neurons in the heart which communicate with the brain. Hormones from the heart travel in our bloodstream. Every time the heart beats, it creates both pulse waves of pressure, and of electromagnetic energy that travel through the body and to the brain. Amazingly, the heart generates a magnetic field 5000 times more powerful than that of the brain. It can be measured six feet away from the body. It almost certainly extends further, but this is the limit of our current sensing equipment.

We all too often forget that the brain is just the most complex end of a whole nervous system which extends throughout our body. For example, the nerves in our hands are in almost constant communication with our brains, a fact that leads some to believe that the ancient art of palm-reading may have some validity: if the nerves on our hands are constantly communicating back and forth with our brains, then it's not an unreasonable stretch of the imagination to wonder if our personalities could imprint themselves on the lines of the skin of our palms. Similarly, our hearts are also in constant communication with our brains. Could a similar effect be occurring with the heart? Could the 10-15% of heart donation recipients who – like Claire Silvia – experience changes in their tastes, personalities and memories be picking up on information on the heart's original owner that was stored in the heart itself?

Gary Schwartz, a professor of psychology and psychiatry at Yale university believes so. He has developed a theory that could explain how the heart learns and remembers. Schwartz points out that all that is required for a system to be able to learn is that it has dynamic feedback: the outputs feed back to the inputs. Any such system that has feedback can learn. As the brain and the heart have feedback – both through neurons and through the bloodstream – the heart can in theory learn. Schwartz, in collaboration with Professor Paul Pearsall, a cardio neurologist from the University of Honalulu (and author of 'The Heart's Code'), collected a number of case studies of heart donation recipients who have experienced these unusual changes. Among them is the case of a 47 year old white man who received the heart of a young black man. Whilst the 47 year old was not racist, he did have a number of underlying assumptions about what kinds of tastes a young black man would have. He joked that if his tastes had changed, perhaps he would now start to like rap music! But what actually happened was the man became obsessed with classical music, and would listen to it over and over. It turned out that the young black man had in fact been a classical violin player. Another heart recipient suddenly became obsessed with competitive cycling and swimming, and began training for, and eventually winning competitions at these sports. One year later he discovered his donor had been an athletic Hollywood stuntman.

Whilst there are a number of scientists and doctors who are now convinced that these types of stories could point to the reality of 'heart memories', there are many who also remain sceptical. They argue that there are alternative explanations.

One explanation that's been put forward for these strange experiences is that the drugs that the person has to take so that their immune system doesn't reject their new transplanted heart (immunosuppressant) are causing some kind of psychological effect that makes a person believe they are accessing memories from the organ, particularly as even having a deceased person's heart in your body might play on your imagination. However, while this explanation would account for having some kind of psychological effect, it doesn't account for the accuracy of the information that such heart recipients have come out with. This accuracy is all the more impressive considering that hospitals maintain a policy of not telling the recipient or their family any of the personal details of who their donor was.

Another theory is that the patient manages to pick up enough information from the medical staff around them to piece together – perhaps even subconsciously – some basic details of their donor. It may even be that conversations that doctors and nurses have while the patient is anesthetized are somehow being absorbed by their mind, below the level of conscious awareness. This is certainly plausible, yet in most of the documented cases it has been confirmed that the surgical team had not discussed patient details whilst performing the operation, and indeed, it would be highly unusual for such a discussion to take place.

There may be many orders of magnitude far fewer neurons in the heart than the brain, but many simple animals such as insects can display intelligent behaviour and memory with a relatively small number of neurons. So perhaps this is also true of our hearts?

The Heart' Mind and Spirit (scientific clarity to date…)

By Professor Mohamed Omar Salem

The concept of mind is of central importance for psychiatrists and psychologists. However, little attention has been paid in most formal textbooks to this important issue, which is usually studied under the section of 'Philosophical aspects of psychiatry/psychology'. The practicing psychiatrist should have some working model of the mind to help him understanding his patient's problems (Salem, 2004). This review discusses some aspects of the components of mind, which is only one step on a long road.

In many cultures throughout history, the heart has been considered the source of emotions, passion, and wisdom. Also, people used to feel that they experienced the feeling or sensation of love and other emotional states in the area of the heart. However, in the past, scientists emphasized the role of the brain in the head as being responsible for such experiences. Interestingly, recent studies have explored physiological mechanisms by which the heart communicates with the brain, thereby influencing information processing, perceptions, emotions and health. These studies provided the scientific basis to explain how and why the heart affects mental clarity, creativity and emotional balance. In this review, I shall try to summarize and integrate the interesting findings in this area.

Heart and emotions

It is long known that changes in emotions are accompanied by predictable changes in the heart rate, blood pressure, respiration, and digestion. Therefore, when we are aroused, the sympathetic division of the autonomic nervous system energizes us for fight or flight, and in more quiet times, the parasympathetic component cools us down. In this view, it was assumed that the autonomic nervous system and the physiological responses moved in concert with the brain's response to a given stimulus (Rein, Atkinson, et al, 1995).

The heart and brain

However, following several years of research, it was observed that, the heart communicates with the brain in ways that significantly affect how we perceive and react to the world. It was found that, the heart seemed to have its own peculiar logic that frequently diverged from the direction of the autonomic nervous system. The heart appeared to be sending meaningful messages to the brain that it not only understood, but also obeyed (Lacey and Lacey, 1978). Later, neurophysiologists discovered a neural pathway and mechanism whereby input from the heart to the brain could inhibit or facilitate the brain's electrical activity (McCraty, 2002).

The brain in the heart:

After extensive research, Armour (1994) introduced the concept of functional 'heart brain'. His work revealed that the heart has a complex intrinsic nervous system that is sufficiently sophisticated to qualify as a 'little brain' in its own right. The heart's brain is an intricate network of several types of neurons, neurotransmitters, proteins, and support cells similar to those found in the brain proper. Its elaborate circuitry enables it to act independently of the cranial brain – to learn, remember, and even feel and sense. The heart's nervous system contains around 40,000 neurons, called sensory neurites (Armour, 1991). Information from the heart - including feeling sensations - is sent to the brain through several afferents. These afferent nerve pathways enter the brain at the area of the medulla, and cascade up into the higher centres of the brain, where they may influence perception, decision- making, and other cognitive processes (Armour, 2004).

Thus, it was revealed that the heart has its own intrinsic nervous system that operates and processes information independently of the brain or nervous system. This is what allows a heart transplant to work. Normally, the heart communicates with the brain via nerve fibres running through the vagus nerve and the spinal column. In a heart transplant, these nerve connections do not reconnect for an extended period; in the meantime, the transplanted heart is able to function in its new host only through the capacity of its intact, intrinsic nervous system (Murphy, et al, 2000)

The heart's magnetic field:

Research has also revealed that the heart communicates information to the brain and throughout the body via electromagnetic field interactions. The heart generates the body's most powerful and most extensive rhythmic electromagnetic field. The heart's magnetic component is about 500 times stronger than the brain's magnetic field and can be detected several feet away from the body. It was proposed that, this heart field acts as a carrier wave for information that provides a global synchronizing signal for the entire body (McCraty, Bradley & Tomasino, 2004)... Heart field interactions between individuals.

There is now evidence that a subtle yet influential electromagnetic or 'energetic' communication system operates just below our conscious awareness. Energetic interactions possibly contribute to the 'magnetic' attractions or repulsions that occur between individuals, and also affect social relationships. It was also found that one person's brain waves can synchronize to another person's heart (McCraty, 2004).

Communication via hormones: the heart as a hormonal gland

Another component of the heart-brain communication system was provided by researchers studying the hormonal system. The heart was reclassified as an endocrine gland when, in 1983, a hormone produced and released by the heart called atrial natriuretic factor (ANF) was isolated. This hormone exerts its effect on the blood vessels, on the kidneys, the adrenal glands, and on a large number of regulatory regions in the brain. It was also found that the heart contains a cell type known as 'intrinsic cardiac adrenergic'' (ICA) cells. Theses cells release noradrenaline and dopamine neurotransmitters, once thought to be produced only by neurons in the CNS. More recently, it was discovered that the heart also secretes oxytocin, commonly referred to as the 'love' or bonding hormone. In addition to its functions in childbirth and lactation, recent evidence indicates that this hormone is also involved in cognition, tolerance, adaptation, complex sexual and maternal behaviours, learning social cues and the establishment of enduring pair bonds. Concentrations of oxytocin in the heart were found to be as high as those found in the brain (Cantin & Genest, 1986).

Increasing psycho physiological coherence data indicate that when heart rhythm patterns are coherent, the neural information sent to the brain facilitates cortical function. This effect is often experienced as heightened mental clarity, improved decision-making, and increased creativity. Additionally, coherent input from the heart tends to facilitate the experience of positive feeling states. This may explain why most people associate love and other positive feelings with the heart and why many people actually feel or sense these emotions in the area of the heart. Therefore, the heart seems to be intimately involved in the generation of psycho physiological coherence (Tille et al, 1996, & McCraty, 2000).

The heart and amygdala

Research has shown that the heart's afferent neurological signals directly affect activity in the amygdala and associated nuclei, an important emotional processing centre in the brain. The amygdala is the key brain centre that coordinates behavioural, immunological, and neuroendocrine responses to environmental threats. It compares incoming emotional signals with stored emotional memories, and accordingly makes instantaneous decisions about the level of perceived threat. Due to its extensive connections to the limbic system, it is able to take over the neural pathways, activating the autonomic nervous system and emotional response before the higher brain centres receive the sensory information (Rein, McCraty and Atkinson, 1995 & McCraty et al, 1995).

The heart and intuition

A very interesting research finding has been that the heart is involved in the processing and decoding of intuitive information (McCraty, Atkinson & Bradley, 2004). Previous data suggests that the heart's field was directly involved in intuitive perception, through its coupling to an energetic information field outside the bounds of space and time (Childre & McCraty, 2001). Using a rigorous experimental design, there was evidence that both the heart and brain receive and respond to information about a future event before the event actually happens. Even more surprising was that the heart appeared to receive this intuitive information before the brain (McCraty, Atkinson & Bradley, 2004).

Discussion

It has long been thought that conscious awareness originates in the brain alone. Recent scientific studies suggest that consciousness emerges from the brain and body acting together (Popper & Eccles, 2000). As has been shown, a growing body of evidence now suggests that the heart plays a particularly significant role in this process. The above findings indicate that, the heart is far more than a simple pump. In fact, it is seen now as a highly complex, self - organizing information processing centre with its own functional 'brain' that communicates with, and influences, the cranial brain via the nervous system, hormonal system, and other pathways. The involvement of the heart with intuitive functions is another interesting piece of information. However, as persons with transplanted hearts can function normally, the heart can be considered here as a medium or tool, for an underlying more sophisticated integrating system that has the capacity to carry the personal identity of the individual.

These new visions might give better understanding to the concept of mind as a multi-component unit that is not only interacting with the physical environment through demonstrable means, but also has the capacity to communicate with the cosmic universe through non-physical pathways (Lorimer, 2001). This gives rise to the concept of the spirit as the non-physical element, or the field, of the mind that can communicate with the cosmos outside the constraints of space and time. The evidence for such communication comes from the reported phenomena of extra - sensory perception (telepathy, precognition, and clairvoyance), psycho-kinesis, psychic healing, and religious experiences (Radin, 1997 & Henry, 2005).

Possibly further advancement in quantum physics may one day give us further insight into how we can formulate this new model of the heart, mind and spirit.

References

1. Armour J A (1991), Anatomy and function of the intrathoracic neurons regulating the mammalian heart. In: Zucker I H and Gilmore J P, eds. Reflex Control of the Circulation. Boca Raton, FL, CRC Press: 1-37.

2. Armour J A (1994), Neurocardiology: Anatomical and Functional Principles, New York, NY, Oxford University Press: 3-19.

3. Armour J. A. (2004), Cardiac neuronal hierarchy in health and disease, American

4. Journal of physiology, regulatory, integrative and comparative physiology. Aug; 287(2):R262-71.

5. Cantin M. and Genest J. (1986), the heart as an endocrine gland, Clinical and Investigative Medicine; 9(4): 319-327.

6. Childre D, McCraty R (2001), Psycho physiological

Correlates of Spiritual Experience, Biofeedback; 29(4):13-17.

7. Henry J (2005), Parapsychology, Routledge, Taylor, and Francis Group: 91- 148.

8. Lacey J I and Lacey B C (1978), Two-way communication between the heart and the brain: Significance of time within the cardiac cycle. American Psychologist, February: 99-113.

9. Lorimer D (2001), Thinking Beyond the Brain: A Wider Science of Consciousness; 34-80. Floris Books, Edinburgh, UK.

10. McCraty R (2000), Psycho physiological coherence: A link between positive emotions, stress reduction, performance, and health. Proceedings of the Eleventh International Congress on Stress, Mauna Lani Bay, Hawaii.

11. McCraty R (2002), Influence of Cardiac Afferent Input on Heart-Brain Synchronization and Cognitive Performance. International Journal of Psychophysiology; 45(1-2):72-73.

12. McCraty R (2004), The Energetic Heart: Bio electromagnetic Communication Within and Between People, Chapter published in: Clinical Applications of Bio electromagnetic Medicine, edited by Rosch P J and Markov M S. New York: Marcel Dekker: 541-562.

13. McCraty R, Atkinson M, Bradley RT (2004, a), Electrophysiological Evidence of Intuition: Part 1. The Surprising Role of the Heart, Journal of Alternative and Complementary Medicine; 10(1):133-143.

14. McCraty R, Atkinson M, Bradley RT (2004, b),

Electrophysiological Evidence of Intuition: Part 2; A System-Wide Process? Journal of Alternative and Complementary Medicine (2004); 10(2):325-336.

15. McCraty R, Atkinson M and Tiller W A et al (1995), The Effects of Emotions on Short-Term Power Spectrum Analysis of Heart Rate Variability. American Journal of Cardiology; 76(14):1089–1093.

16. McCraty R, Bradley RT, Tomasino D (2004), The Resonant Heart, Shift: At the Frontiers of Consciousness; 5:15-19.

17. Murphy D A, Thompson G W, et al (2000), The heart reinnervates after transplantation. Annals of Thoracic Surgery; 69(6): 1769-1781.

18. Popper K and Eccles J C (2000), The Self-Conscious Mind and the Brain. In: The Self and Its Brain. Routledge, Taylor & Francis Group, London and New York: 355-376

19. Radin D I (1997), The Conscious Universe: The Scientific Truth of Psychic Phenomena, Harper Edge, San Francisco, 1997: 61-174.

20. Rein G, Atkinson M, et al (1995), The physiological and psychological effects of compassion and anger. Journal of Advancement in Medicine; 8(2): 87-105.

21. Rein G, McCraty R and Atkinson M (1995), The Physiological and Psychological Effects of Compassion and Anger, Journal of Advancement in Medicine; 8(2):87–105.

22. Salem, MO (2004) The Necessity to Review Psychiatric Curricula, e-Community; International Journal of Mental Health & Addiction, Mental Health Care in the Gulf Conference Proceedings.

23. Tiller W, McCraty R, et al (1996), Cardiac coherence; A new non-invasive measure of autonomic system order. Alternative Therapies in Health and Medicine; 2(1): 52-65.

24. American Heart Association. "Heart Transplantation." 2002. MedLine Plus. 20 Nov. 2002. <www.nlm.nih.gov>. This website provides some statistics concerning heart transplantation and survival rates.

25. Bellecci, Pauline M., MD. "The Heart Remembers." 2002. The Natural Connection. 12 Nov. 2002. <http://www.thenaturalconnection.net>.

26. Carroll, Robert Todd. "Cellular Memory." 2002. The Skeptics Dictionary. Nov. 12 2002. <http://skepdic.com/cellular.html>.

27. Hawthorne, Peter. The Transplanted Heart. Chicago: Rand McNally & Company. 1968.

28. McGoon, Michael D., M.D. Mayo Clinic Heart Book, New York, William Morrow and Company, Inc. 1993.

29. Merriam-Webster Online. "Psychotropic." 2003. Merriam-Webster, Inc. 25 January 2003. <http://www.m-w.com>.

30. Pearsall, Paul, The Heart's Code, New York, Broadway Books, 1998.

31. Pert, Candace, Why do we feel the way we feel? The Seer. 3 Dec. 2002. <http://www.angelfire.com/hi/TheSeer/Pert.html>.

32. Sylvia, Claire, A Change of Heart, Boston: Little, Brown and Company. 1997

Freedom comes when you take instructions first from your heart and not from your head. It is heartfullness, with a small amount of headiness. You will need to strengthen and maybe build your muscle for doing this. It, may be weak or may have only been used in crises when, without a point of reference, we are forced to get into the moment, because we must. Why wait until you are in crisis mode to access this heartfullness?

Humans are not designed to think for too long. Excessive thinking actually puts our physical body under immense pressure and we stop breathing properly. Observe others and yourself when you worry. We literally stop breathing! We need to breathe to stay alive. Stop breathing and you kill yourself far more quickly than through lack of food or water – we are literally dead within minutes. How can one feel healthy or be resourceful when we drastically reduce our breathing particularly as we continue to abuse and yet, at the same time, always demand the most from our body!

Our breathing and water intake are critical for survival. Forget diet for now, let us just focus on breathing and water intake, both are crucial and yet underrated. A lack of these causes us problems and even major health issues in the short and long term. Without them, we have far less energy, are much less resourceful, and struggle to do the necessities let alone deal with the major challenges that come our way. To properly function and make better decisions we need to breathe and to drink more live water.

Constant head spinning isolates us, cutting us off from our true selves and everything else around us adding to our misery. I know because I have been there. Once we become aware of our thoughts, we can free ourselves from the isolation of our delusions.

We were never designed to be lonely. We can be alone, absolutely. It is important to be alone, but being lonely is not in our design. Otherwise everything in the universe wouldn't be so connected including the soil we walk on, which was once someone's sister, brother, father and where our own body will eventually return. The food at our tables, the cars we drive, the homes we live in, the clothes on our backs all link us back to each other. All of us are part of the cycle of life, now and forever. We are never alone, as we are all connected by genuine love and care.

This connection becomes clear when we function at our best and are in touch with our true self. For example, we see a stranger fall in the street we automatically kick into action, forgetting our own worries, and go to their rescue without even thinking! This is in our nature, because we are connected and we genuinely care, despite our mind-led stranger and ego trying to disconnect us through excessive thinking!

Live a day in shorter time spans and take worries away.

It is amazing how life is so much less heavy if one lives by thinking in shorter time spans. Engaging with what we feel about things, rather than thinking, takes the pressure off. It also makes us access our true selves more easily, we engage more frequently and in doing so, we use all our senses to make better decisions and live life in the present!

Imagine you are making your usual plans but then start only planning in 30 minutes to 1-hour time spans. Plan without pressure or judgement, nor analysis. Your whole purpose of living is captured in whatever you are doing in those short time spans. I promise your mind will stop being bored, it will be difficult to worry about too much else, as your mind, will have taken full charge of you again!

Your mind has a purpose again which means you can take action immediately as you are doing something purposeful for you. It also has an amazing healing transformation and in addition you will get to breathe deeply once again.

"Some men see things as they are and say why? I dream things that never were and say why not?" **R.F Kennedy**

Paul Fashade B.SC, M.A.

An important true story...

In 1871 a young Canadian man read 21 words in a book that changed his life. He was a medical student at Montreal General Hospital. He was stressed about passing his final exams and later where to build up a practise and how to create a living from it.

Those 21 words helped to make him one of the greatest icons of modern medicine and he was later knighted for his services to medicine. His most famous work 'The Principles and Practice of Medicine' quickly became a key text for both students and physicians alike. His name was Sir William Osler. The 21 words he read were from Thomas Carlyle. They enabled him to learn to live worry free for most of his life.

"Our main business is not to see what lies dimly at a distance, but to do what lies clearly at hand"

42 years later, in a speech one spring night to students of Yale university, Sir William Osler confessed that as a professor of 4 different universities and having published a seminal text he was considered to have "brains of special quality". His confession was that this was simply not true. However, he had developed the ability to ask himself questions that seek out the truth. Sir William Osler said that his close friends who knew him well would agree his brain was "of the most mediocre character".

So, what enabled Sir William to live a worry free life? What was his secret? A few months earlier, Sir William had crossed the Atlantic on a great ocean liner where he watched the captain press buttons that would automatically shut off various parts of the ship and create watertight compartments. He explained how he lived in "day-tight compartments":

"Now each one of you is a much more marvellous organisation than the ocean liner and bound for a longer voyage. What I urge is that you learn to control the machinery as to live in 'day- tight compartments' as this is the

most certain way to ensure safety on the voyage. Get on the bridge and see that at least the great bulkheads are in working order. Touch a button and hear, at every level of your life, the iron doors shutting out the past – the dead yesterdays. Touch another button and shut off, with a metal curtain, the future – unborn tomorrows. Then you are safe – safe for today!! .... Shut off the past!! Let the dead past bury its dead…shut out the yesterdays which have lighted fools the way to dusty death!! .... The load of tomorrow, added to that of yesterday, carried today, makes the strongest falter. Shut off the future as tightly as the past…. The future is today…there is no tomorrow. The day of a man's (or a woman's) salvation is now. Waste of energy, mental distress, nervous worries dog the steps of a man (or woman) who is anxious about the future…shut close, then, the great fore and aft bulkheads, and prepare to cultivate the habit of a life of 'day-tight compartments."

He is not saying never plan for tomorrow but remember that a plan is only, at best a good guide. Rarely does anything go exactly to plan, something always changes. We have all experienced this. It is without doubt enjoyable, purposeful, and rewarding to put all one's effort, enthusiasm, and energy into doing today's work in the moment. It has worked wonders for me all my life. I get enthused and inspired to do and create when I put my deep interest and pay full attention to whatever I am doing in that moment.

In the past when my heart was not truly engaged in something, I could not hide my lack of interest, and I always paid the price. Sometimes being my true self would mean not being popular, not fitting in with the rules or the boundaries of a system or organisation. As a result, I did not enjoy most of my previous work experiences, I disliked following rules that did not make much sense to me. Like most people do, I compromised at the time, using the need for money to justify doing the job. I convinced myself I needed the nice holidays, the enjoyable lifestyle. But then came a point when I could no longer justify it anymore. I had to search within for my own truth. This path I was leading did not give me any satisfaction or personal genuine power, in fact it was literally killing me inside. I told myself, that if I wanted to feel differently about myself and have a different set of circumstances then I had better begin to create them.

So what did I do? What enabled me to get out of this all too familiar frustrating situation? What kicked me into action was making a list of my heartfelt answers to those important questions. I did not allow myself any 'buts' or 'maybes' but I just acted upon them.

One can only pretend for so long as you know you will just get miserable in the end and other people will see and feel it, as they know that your heart is not really in it. I only have so many summers and winters to go so I should be sure to live my heart-felt truth. I do not want to leave with regrets or a heavy heart! I want my heart and mind to stay light and open. I will be fully aware until the last second of my life. I will be speaking my truth and staying free in love with life, and everything in it that creates my experience and allows me to grow. This I am certain of, without doubt, as I have done it long enough to trust myself, and my courage flows from this naturally.

All things (people, the universe) conspire to help you and so your ability to create increases even more. This is not guesswork on my part, or spiritual "blah blah", it will unquestionably happen to you, you just need to connect to your truth and genuine self, and your courage will flow from that. Then things will come to you more naturally and you will stop thinking of worries as problems instead they will become challenges enabling you to find a way to solve them, without excessive thinking.

When people engage with their genuine true self then impossible things become possible whereas those who don't follow their heart and senses will still see them as impossible as they are not yet ready to experience their true natural gifted self. They are still following others and running on conditioned scripts! As they do not respond naturally, and they are led by fear and worry, so their journey is usually reactive rather than responsive.

Nothing waits for us; time nor opportunities. They slip through our fingers like sand in an hourglass. Most people don't like to look back over their past as they feel they have failed in some way. They see their life as short, unfair and uneventful. Life may be short but it is nothing to be afraid of. The question is, are we going to live on our own terms, being true to ourselves, with self-awareness or delay our true-life calling and live in fear? Time will surely pass through us whether we choose to answer that question or not.

Imagine that you realised that you only have 20 more holidays left to take, how would you live your life towards these holidays, where would you go, and what would you do differently? Would you still go to the same place at the same time every year?

Let us consider our lifestyle, the way we treat our body, and most importantly how we are living our truth without forgetting and learning from our past? If you are doing what you love, listening to one's heart and living one's truth most of the time, then you can die unafraid, fully satisfied that you have lived your life.

Do not wait until it is too late to turn around and take a different route – start on your new path early. I speak from experience, when I had my wakeup call or kick up the ass I very quickly aligned with my heart's choices and my head followed. This is what I call my heart's true blue print and knowing.

I had a horrible car crash in my early 20s that took me just over 3 years to fully recover from. When my time came close, it was completely unannounced and unexpected! When I had the crash, just before I lost consciousness, I recall thinking the worst, being afraid, and swearing loudly! But long after I came around, I relived that moment several times and realised this must never happen to me again. I never wanted to feel so damned afraid and lost!

Why was I so afraid? I realised that I was afraid because I had not even begun living my heartfelt choices. In addition, my body was

totally unprepared as I had been abusing it from all directions. In short, my body and mind were totally ego-led and so was everyone around me.

My self-awareness and self-esteem were very low; my life was being conditioned by what I thought I was supposed to do! I knew it was bullshit but I could not pull myself away from those things even though I knew they were not making me happy. I thought I needed to attend university, have the cool job, earn lots of money, and buy all the latest gadgets and life's toys to amuse myself.

I realised that I had been justifying my actions because I wanted to fit in or be loved but deep down I was not listening or responding to what truly made me happy and learning to do that more often.

When we put love into it and listen to our heart's truth then we can begin our own mastery. Once you open that door, you will begin to feel alive, feel free and like you are finally singing your song. It is true that when one is doing what one loves or finds deeply interesting, your heart will be fully connected with your natural self and you will be in your zone.

Every one of us can live our truth. It is not for a select few. Do not convince yourself or believe that it is impossible for you. We are all capable of reaching our truth and choosing to live by it.

Let me repeat myself, this is not just for a select few, not just for great leaders, scientists, artists, pop stars, singers, models etc. Just ask yourself how they got there in the first place?

The beautiful words below helped me through many tough times in my life. They bring me back to myself and remind me of who I used to be and the incredible person I am now and the things that I have done no matter how simple, big or small. I bet you have also done similar things, even if you somehow choose not to remember!

This quotation helps me listen to my truth regardless of my worries or pressures during my difficult hours, but also when I'm celebrating, so I never forget what is possible even when I've been told I was crazy to even try! Nelson Mandela famously used these words when he spoke to the people of Cape Town at his inauguration. They are in fact the beautiful words of Marianne Williamson:

"Our deepest fear is not that we are inadequate. Our deepest fear is that we are powerful beyond measure. It is our light, not our darkness that most frightens us. We ask ourselves, who am I to be brilliant, gorgeous, talented, and fabulous? Actually, who are you not to be? You are a child of God. Your playing small does not serve the world. There is nothing enlightened about shrinking so that other people do not feel insecure around you. We are all meant to shine, as children do. We were born to make manifest the glory of God that is within us. It is not just in some of us; it is in everyone. And as we let our own light shine, we unconsciously give other people permission to do the same. As we are liberated from our own fear, our presence automatically liberates others."

The idea of being scared of my own growth, success, and enlightenment always gives me clarity of thought and so I ask myself:

- What if this was actually true?

- Who am I now? And what would I become in the future if I keep sabotaging myself?

- How have my excuses served me to date? If I am brutally honest? And who will I become if I truly do nothing and keep justifying my fears, so I stand still?

- What do I feel my sincere truth is in all this, no pressure, just guess, if I do not know?

- What must I do from now just to make it better? Make a list, and keep asking what else?

- Who would I become if I just make it a little better from now?

- Who could I become in the future if I did not have these unhelpful thoughts anymore?

- What do I feel I would honestly do if I had no more blocks or limitations, just guessing, with no pressure?

Asking myself these questions saved my life in more ways than one. They remain my checklist for getting back whenever I feel lost or whenever I am worrying. No more doubts. This is easily achievable. It just needs practice, repetition and do not forget, it also needs to be fun!

Some of us have almost forgotten how to play, as we have become adults, indeed some resort to drugs to feel happy or playful. Sir William Osler encouraged everybody, including the students at Yale to begin each day with Christ's prayer: *"Give us this day our daily bread".* You don't need to believe in God to use this but notice how this is such a simple request rather than "Oh God, there's been so little rain in the wheat belt and we may have another drought –then how will I get bread to eat next year- or suppose I lose my business – or suppose I lose my job – oh, God, how could I get bread then?"

I personally believe in a greater being but you do not need to believe in any God or universal power, as you will find your truth in whatever resonates with you. I have talked a lot about achieving the seeming impossible. Think about those individuals who created all those wonderfully impossible inventions like electricity, the mobile phone, planes, the Internet etc. They were created or developed by both believers and non-believers to help create more abundance for you and others. This proves that it does not really matter which faith inspires or kicks you into spirit or living with your true self. **When** we are inspired which means in spirit, we do great things, beyond thinking and logic or reason.

What we think or analyse to death generally loses its usefulness to us, the more we think about it. Usually our initial instinct, or heartfelt guide is probably more relevant or useful to us. We can have wonderful intellectual conversations and may impress others, but are only really distracting ourselves.

I truly enjoy toys and treats (houses, cars, travels, gadgets that make life easy, great food and more), but I will not trade my soul or spirit, or heart's calling for them. Interestingly enough, when you truly go with your heart's courage the toys come effortlessly anyway. Remember the disciplined dog that continued chasing its tail whilst the street dog just followed his or her heart and his tail just followed the dog around everywhere he or she goes.

When we listen to our heart's choice, with interest and finally walk our path, we end up truly living our lives shining, regardless of the challenges that may come. Now do you still believe it is better to stay in the shadows and wait for death?

In order to really access ourselves, we must genuinely start by looking at the raw truth without blame, judgement or excessive analysis. Only then can we really check our thoughts that make us full of fear and worry to deeply see if they are still true for us. I hope I do not appear cynical because it is certainly not my intention. But I have explored and become aware of so many issues through my own life, including through coaching and training many people, both radically and gently. I've also observed so many individuals in all walks of life, even those fighting on the front line in the UK armed forces and it has made me realise that most still listen and talk to their thinking analytical logical minds.

Our past history will be our past history and we can lay to rest our old habits and create new ones. The old data in our thinking no longer serves us so we need to create new images and stories that do help us. Why do we hold onto our past history and old data that no longer serves us? What makes this so? Please be truthful in your answers! When was the last time you asked for an updated version of yourself? We all like to have the latest model mobile phone, or TV but seem to forget to get an updated version of something much more important – ourselves!

Some simple, useful and yet powerful key questions…

The main message in this chapter is to live within one day or short time compartments. Shut the iron doors on the past and the future and only focus your interest, intelligence and enthusiasm on the task at hand. Basically what you are doing in any 'now' moment.

Important Exercise:

Please answer truthfully from your heart:

1. What do I feel must happen honestly for me to live in shorter time compartments?

2. What do I feel must happen just to make my situation simply better?

3. What 3 things must I do from now to regret less from the past, things that I simply cannot go back and change?

4. What do I feel will work better for myself - to live easily in the present and worry less about the future?

5. What must happen for me to get up each morning determined to "seize the day" for just this next 24 hours only?

6. What else do I feel I must do, to get more out of my life "living in day-tight compartments in your inner home?"

7. What exactly must happen for me to start immediately?

8. What specific date will I actually start without fooling myself? If I am truly honest?

We think we do not have time, we do! If you think you do not get an audio recorder and play with the 4 simple questions below, to shift you in a direction that will work for you. I have often worked with these questions and they greatly help me empty my worries out and actually solving problems quicker. They truly help you observe your mind, and rid you of your worries and move you to action, and resolve, no BS...here they are:

Q 1: What is the worst thing that could ever happen in this situation?

If your brain replies I do not know because it is trying to avoid the question, just tell yourself *'I know I do not know, and that is ok. But, I'm going to just guess anyway, with no pressure.'* Or put another way, *I know I do not know, but if I were to guess, what would it truly be, again with no pressure?*

These questions are designed to playback with your brain and your 'mind-led stranger' that is always trying to keep you in the drama, so you stay locked in and cannot move. I have used these questions so many times with so many people and they get amazing results. I promise it works like a dream providing you are brutally honest with your answers!

Try it and see. You will get a response that is true to you. This is the beginning of self-truth and self-trust. This is how you develop those weak muscles with your senses and mind that have never really been used before. You can also ask a friend or someone that is close to you to ask you these questions. You just need to answer genuinely and boldly without holding back. You will not be disappointed and you have a hell of a lot to gain. Besides, what is the worst that could happen, you can only go back to worrying right?! Enjoy the process...

A must exercise if you are freaking out or panicking in your head thoughts!

Take a couple of deep breaths, if you get upset or are unsettled, especially when short of breath in that state!

If you just cannot break the mind-led stranger's drama, then do something silly, funny or just scream, laugh or jump up and down! Do anything that is completely out of character for you. I kid you not; it will stop you dead in your drama, so you can get back to yourself and move in the direction that actually helps you.

Q 2: Is it fair to say that I cannot change what has just happened? Can I really go backwards? How can I accept it and just make it a little better for now?

This first question is intentionally silly – of course everyone knows that we cannot go backwards and change things but it alerts us to the ridiculousness in trying to think we can. Your mind-led stranger is like a child that needs lots of attention, because he or she has nothing else to do, it will start playing with you. It knows it will get more attention from you when it bugs you the most through your fearful thoughts and we fall for it every time! So we must discipline and clear our mind of dialogues that just do not help us, period! Make your mind realise you are on to it, any which way you can.

What is the worst thing that could happen to you? Hmmm... you might just feel better and solve your problems and move forward.

Q 3: What must I do to just make it better from now?

This question is very important and intentionally simple so that there is no need for self-analysis or self-judgement. You are your own expert, no one knows you better than you. It is time to be your own best friend for a change!

Once again, if the answer in your head is I do not know, then, say to yourself…I know I do not know, and that is ok, so what would I guess, no pressure?

Make sure you record it or write it down, capture it for observation. This is crucial in getting rid of those unhelpful thoughts and quietening your mind-led stranger.

Q 4: What must happen for me to put a lot of enthusiasm and heart into just making it better?

Again, another simple question that makes it easier to shift you towards a resolution, and move you towards what helps you creatively, mentally, and physically. You will also find this process very healing.

CHAPTER 4

THE JOY OF WORRYING…!

Those who do not know how to calm their worries, simply die sooner.

Even the great Nobel Prize winner for medicine, Dr Alexis Carrel, said, "businessmen who do not know how to fight worry die young" And so does everyone else that stays or lives there frequently. Where do you spend most of your time?

We really do not have to go very far to see the side effects of worrying, just check out those around you. There will be those who have had nervous breakdowns, those who have had heart attacks, those that suffer from anxiety attacks or any manner of illnesses brought on by stress. Of course, we all know deep down that there is nothing like stress, only stressful thoughts.

I am just stating how it is clearly and plainly, we all know what pictures, movies, and sounds we are running in our minds. However, in our movie we have the power to re-write our script and may even get an Oscar in life for being finally original, such as the great people that inspire us.

In New Mexico, Dr O.F. Gober, the chief physician of the Gulf of Colorado and Santa Fe Hospital Association said: *"70% of all patients who come to physicians could cure themselves if they only got rid of their fears and worries. Don't think for a moment that I mean that their illnesses are imaginary…their illnesses are real. I know what I am talking about…for I myself suffered from a stomach ulcer for twelve years. Fear causes worry. Worry makes you tense and nervous and affects the nerves of your stomach and actually changes the gastric juices of your stomach and often leads to stomach ulcers."*

Dr. Joseph F. Montague, author of the book Nervous Stomach Trouble, concurs… he said: *"you do not get stomach ulcers from what you eat. You get ulcers from what is eating you."*

We know this already, as our body constantly sends us loud uncomfortable messages that we ignore or temporarily shut up with some quick fix like a tablet but of course it builds up and reappears in a bigger way and could even be life threatening.

Dr W. C. Alvarez, of Mayo Clinic, said, "ulcers frequently flare up or subside according to the hills and valleys of emotional stress". This was backed up by a study of 15,000 patients treated for stomach disorders at the Mayo Clinic: "4 out of 5 had no physical cause for their stomach illnesses. Fear, worry, hate, selfishness, and the inability to adjust themselves to the world of reality were largely the causes of their stomach illnesses and stomach ulcers."

There was another paper, one of many presented at the annual meeting of the American Association of Industrial Physicians and Surgeons. This paper looked at a study by Dr Harold C. Habein of the Mayo Clinic of 176 business executives with an average age was 44 years. Slightly more than a third of these executives reported that they had suffered from at least 1 of 3 ailments peculiar to high-tension living; heart disease, digestive-tract ulcers, and high blood pressure. There were similar findings made in studies in the UK.

Is it possible to call it business progress and success, if the only way it can be achieved is through chasing it with stomach problems, heart issues, and migraines or constant headaches?

What shall it profit a man if he gains the whole world but loses his health?

So I say seek out what your heart wills leaving the rest alone behind you. My record of sick leave with old employers proves this - doing a job I completely disliked for money or just to pay my bills or satisfy my ego, or buy more toys, was what my life amounted to. I am sure many can relate to this – excessive repeated sickness is a clear sign from your body, as are those days you take off sick because you just do not want to go to work. I know for certain that when I enjoy my job nothing, not even sickness will keep me away nor will it hang around long enough to stop me doing what I love to do. What about you? Be honest?

When I have problems with what I enjoy doing or love they become challenges rather than a worrying pain in the ass! However, when you are doing something you dislike, a problem means anxiety and dread accompanied by that sickening feeling deep in the stomach. We do not really need a doctor to confirm it, we feel it and know ourselves in our body, don't we? I would recommend a book by Dr. Edward Podolsky, entitled 'Stop Worrying and Get Well'. I would like to share the chapter titles with you now:

- What Worry Does to Your Heart
- High Blood Pressure is Fed by Worry
- Rheumatism Can be Caused By Worry
- Worry Less For Your Stomach's Sake
- How Worry Can Cause a Cold
- Worry and The Thyroid
- The Worrying Diabetic

Need I say more? This book is about the courage to find your own truth and asking those questions you never had the courage to ask before!

Even Doctor Russell L. Cecil, a world-recognised authority on arthritis, has listed 4 of the most common conditions that bring on arthritis:

1. Marital shipwreck

2. Financial disaster and grief

3. Loneliness and worry

4. Long-cherished resentments (our dreaded past history!!).

Arthritis does not just appear without a cause! Of course, there are different kinds of arthritis, derived from various causes, but these are the most common cited by Dr. Russell L. Cecil. Do you know what this means? Worry can literally put you in a wheelchair with rheumatism and arthritis. If we stop worrying so much and rather than playing with our wishbone, instead strengthen our backbone, this will build up our courage, allow us to get to know our self better while listening more to our body. This is the key to anything we seek!

I recently read that medical researchers are working on a vaccine for high blood pressure, anxiety attacks and other similar physical reactions spawned by worry. People are taking pills inappropriately. "It has virtually no side effects", now where have you heard that before? That is fine if you are happy to give your life over to "experts" and take no responsibility yourself to find a more natural preventive way. We need to take a more active approach to listening and responding to our bodies. We treat our body like it is useless, forgetting that its sole purpose, design and build is to keep us alive, and nourish us with energy, and provide us with resources to do what we want without too much resistance. However, eventually our 'buddy' can no longer cope and it gives up on us.

What makes it so difficult for us to trust our body? Don't you have a relationship with your body? We are aware when we have a headache or stomach ache but for anything else we run straight to the drug experts with the white coats. I am not trying to undermine doctors here who all genuinely try to help people. One of my close friends in America, who is a renowned doctor, frequently tries to get people to use pretty basic alternative remedies e.g. drink more water to reduce headaches. His patients tell him that if they wanted that kind of advice they would rather not pay Medicare but instead listen to their grandmother! In fact, most insist on being given drugs, that is how bad it is! They may even threaten to sue if they do not get the drugs they want. This is your body. Just because it does not speak to you in words, does not mean it is not speaking to you.

First, one needs to start trusting what we feel or sense from within our body. Start to find a preventative solution rather than always looking for a quick fix or a bottle of pills. In many cases, it is as though we treat our beloved dogs and cats better than we treat ourselves.

I still find it really shocking when I work with people that do not see any value in their lives whatsoever. Yet when I put them on a ledge and ask them to jump, even with a safe landing at the bottom, they definitively choose not to - they want to live. Pole climbing, sky jumping or similar activities are great exercises to awaken individuals, shake off their fears or blocks, and accelerate their learning. For those individuals who do take the jump, they feel so exhilarated and alive. They make the shift and leave their fears behind. It never ceases to amaze people what taking that can achieve. So just jump into life! Believe me your eyes and heart will be wide open to feel yourself again!

Let me give you another analogy; if you break a leg, or badly cut yourself, the pain or blood will force you to fix the problem straight away. Imagine what would happen if you did nothing?! You might not be able to properly walk again or maybe even bleed to death. Now what is the difference between a physical pain in a leg and a 'break' in your mind? Failing to resolve your disturbed mind is equally bad. I do not know about you, but it is not ok for me to carry on being so careless with my mind for so long that I end up hurting myself badly. We all know and truly believe that a cheerful mental state helps the body fight and protect us. This is not just about positive thinking; it is about giving our "buddy" (after all our body is our true best friend) a fighting chance.

I wrote these words to a friend sometime ago but they still remain so relevant today:

> **Only when we do what we love and listen to our heart's will: "I fully sense it my friend, it will always be around and beyond our thinking. It will take its own wonderful shape like the stars in the sky shining in different directions for many other eyes to see and experience. It's called love, and it starts with self love.... finally the start of human social profit"**
>
> **When we first return to ourselves, then we return to love and our courage. This comes from our heart, if we listen and respond. We have grander things beyond our thinking. I promise you it will surprise you, as it does me, and now I accept it as part of my gifts that I play with. We must stop waiting for permission from the world to shine. We must be our own star. I know it is challenging because we have allowed ourselves to be redesigned...like a stone, losing its brilliance. But, we must trust ourselves.**

This is all simply about love of one's self, through courage. Then miracles will happen constantly thereafter. Things our heads or minds cannot explain. We just start living in the unknown, unafraid, where the real juice of life is! Things just open up to us as we finally use the key that has been given to us all at birth. Is this what you thought it would be and feel like? If yes, well done! If no, it is time to find your own truth and know the genuine side of your nature. What do you have to lose? If it does not work for you, you can always go back to doing what you did before. I really doubt you will be disappointed. Just start with something small at first... just take the first step, that is it!

CHAPTER 5

CRUCIAL WAYS TO GET BACK IF YOU THINK YOU HAVE NO TIME!

I want to suggest some simple, practical things that can be done to get back to your genuine self quicker without the fuss or drama! Since so many people say they do not have enough time.

First and foremost let's remember what we use to do, but have forgotten, using some simple questions to help us remember…

What makes me very quickly feel good when I do it?

Now list them and keep asking what else? When nothing comes and if you feel blocked and your mind replies I don't know, (this usually means I can't be bothered), then ask or say to yourself: 'I know I don't know and this is fine, so let me just guess, under no pressure'. It will come to you, just wait a little…

Take no more than 5 minutes to write down a list of 'must do' things… use and do the ones that feel good to you!

When you have tried it, answer the questions by yourself and write down your response. I know it will surprise you and you will learn a hell of a lot from it and discover many unseen advantages. It will make you wonder why you were not taught this earlier in life whether at school or university.

1. Breathing:

This sounds simple enough, right? But did you know that we never use the full capacity of our lungs. We usually use only about 6% to 30% of our total lung capacity. We mainly shallow breathe which in effect means we are running on less than half energy for most of our lives. We also continue to demand more from our body although it is only operating at 50% capacity through lack of breath and also lack of water. In effect our bodies are nearly always under resourced.

You can also do activities such as yoga, jogging, meditation, dancing and sex to naturally stimulate and deepen your body's knowledge of deeper breathing. It is highly healing, produces high energy levels, and will make you feel more alive. It is so crucial to consciously breathe. Although our body will naturally breathe for us, we generally restrict it through our physiology e.g. the way we shrink our posture. Observe yourself and others to ensure you are not blocking your breathing by your posture or by the way you are sitting. By extending outwards, rather than shrinking inwards, you will open up your pathway of breath. Deeper and stronger breaths have an unrestricted quality not only to energy levels within your body but also with your thoughts. When your body is open and unrestricted you will have fewer fears and worries.

Be fully aware of your body positioning, and posture and try to minimise your leak of energy. Deep breaths also improve cell tissues and the faster regeneration of cells as well as help ageing rather than shallow breathing which leads to the degeneration of cell tissues.

Please, also ask yourself these important deeper questions, and again write out your raw responses, without judgement, blame or analysis.

1. What do I genuinely feel happens to me when I restrict my breathing by shrinking my posture, such as through unhelpful thinking?

2. How do I feel while shrinking or when I physically block myself? How does my mind feel while in this posture? Think back and remember.

3. What do I feel really happens when I slow down my breathing or stop altogether, such as during worrying thoughts? What do you observe is the quality of your breath? Think back and remember.

4. How exactly do I feel when I breathe deeply? Try it now and then answer the question. What do I feel makes it a must for me to breathe consciously?

5. How do I honestly feel when I am having stressful thoughts?

6. What else do I feel I can become in the future if I consciously breathe?

Nadi Shodhana Breathing Technique

The good news is the Nadi Shodhana breathing technique is incredibly easy to learn and practice. It is a great pre-cursor to a meditation practice, hatha yoga practice, or even sleep. Outlined below are some guidelines to follow. Start using the Nadi Shodhana Panayama technique and bring balance and vitality back to your life.

Preparation

- Blow your nose to clear any blockages.
- Find a comfortable seat. Preferably, sit cross-legged on the floor, although a chair will do if necessary but make sure your spine is completely erect.

- Keep your mouth closed but make sure your jaw is relaxed.
- Close your eyes and gently gaze at a point in between your eyes. Do not stare, just gently gaze.

Practice

1. Using your left hand, bring your middle and index finger together to a spot touching your forehead between your eyes.
2. Close your LEFT nostril with your thumb.
3. Exhale for 8 seconds from your RIGHT nostril.
4. Inhale for 4 seconds from your RIGHT nostril.
5. Hold your breath for 6 seconds
6. Close your RIGHT nostril with your ring finger and exhale from your LEFT nostril for 8 seconds.
7. Hold with your lungs empty for 2 seconds.
8. Inhale from your LEFT nostril for 4 seconds.
9. Hold the breath for 6 seconds.
10. Close the LEFT nostril with the thumb and exhale from the RIGHT nostril for 8 seconds.
11. Hold with your lungs empty for 2 seconds
12. Inhale with the RIGHT nostril for 4 seconds…and so on…. go back to step 5 and keep repeating the cycle for 2-3 minutes.

2. To be hugged or touched by someone other than your pet!

"A new study from researchers in Utah finds that a warm touch, the non-sexual, supportive kind, tempers stress and blood pressure, adding to a growing body of research on how emotions affect health. The study of 34 young married couples ages 20 to 39 by researchers at Brigham Young University in Provo and the University of Utah in Salt Lake City found that massage and other supportive and caring touch lower stress hormones and blood pressure, particularly among men, while also enhancing oxytocin, a hormone thought to calm and counter stress. The journal Psychosomatic Medicine." By Sharon Jayson, USA TODAY.

Consider the following:

- *Skin-to-skin contact between mother and infant has been shown to benefit the baby's physical development and contributes to a positive attachment relationship between the two. The practice of placing a diaper-clad infant skin-to-skin on the mother is so beneficial that it is now an intervention strategy for premature babies in neonatal intensive care units worldwide.*

- A group of Korean infants under the care of an orphanage were provided with an extra 15 minutes of stimulation twice a day, 5 days a week, for 4 weeks. The additional stimulation consisted of auditory (female voice), tactile (massage), and visual (eye-to-eye contact). Compared to the infants who only received regular care, the stimulated orphans gained significantly more weight and had larger increases in body length and head circumference after the 4-week intervention period, as well as at 6 months of age. In addition, the stimulated infants had fewer illnesses and clinic visits.

- Gentle touch has been shown to facilitate physical and psychological functioning, particularly in terms of reducing stress, relieving pain, increasing the ability to cope, and general health ratings.

- Participants in a study examining the effectiveness of therapeutic touch as a treatment for managing pain, due to fibromyalgia, experienced a significant decrease in pain and reported a significant improvement in quality of life.

- The majority of nursing home residents suffering from dementia, like Alzheimer's disease, develop behavioural symptoms of dementia, such as restlessness, searching and wandering, tapping and banging, pacing and walking, and vocalization. Current treatment involves drugs, but a recent study showed that intervention consisting of therapeutic touch significantly reduces these behavioural symptoms. Impressive is that the therapeutic touch employed in the study was only provided twice per day, for three days. Each therapeutic intervention lasted only 5-7 minutes. Clearly, the importance of touch cannot be underestimated. Applying this knowledge in your closest relationships can make all the difference with your health.

The above passages were taken from the following research and articles below: Understanding Your Partner's Primary Love Language References Browne, J. (2004). Early relationship environments: physiology of skin-to-skin contact for parents and their preterm infants. Clinics In Perinatology, 31(2): 287-98. Denison, B. (2004). Touch the pain away: new research on therapeutic touch and persons with fibromyalgia syndrome. Holistic Nursing Practice, 18(3): 142-51. Kim, T., Shin, Y., & White-Traut, R. (2003). Multisensory intervention improves physical growth and illness rates in Korean orphaned newborn infants. Research in Nursing and Health, 26(6): 424-33. Weze, C., et al. (2005). Evaluation of healing by gentle touch. Public Health, 119(1): 3-10. Wood, D., Craven, R., & Whitney, J. (2005). The effect of therapeutic touch on behavioural symptoms of persons with dementia. Alternative Therapies in Health and Medicine, 11(1): 66-74.

We often love and are more comfortable with dogs, cat, plants, flowers etc and whilst they bring a lot of joy to our lives, they cannot always totally calm you down or reach deeper levels the way that other humans can. To hug or be touched needs to happen more frequently. It is very natural to sincerely crave to be touched and we secretly love it! Then it must be done more often. Touch has an amazing healing power to it, to the core of cells, and this power has always been understated. Let us start with genuine hugs daily, even guys… yes, even us guys. Even a manly sports hug will do as a start!

Remember, when in an embrace with another, your breathing slows down and there exists a peaceful calm. It is impossible to be angry while in an embrace, as there is no space for it. What do I feel is the genuine benefit of being hugged or touched in a nice way daily? What do I feel it really does to my body and mind? How does it make me come back to myself or be more aware? Who must I become to attract being touched the way I desire to be touched? What do I feel must happen to make this better?

3. Smile - the light that connects and laughter that awakens life!

Remember how it makes you feel when you just genuinely smile or someone else smiles at you. To smile, let alone laugh, changes how one feels almost immediately. It has already been wired into our system to switch on our feelings - a kind of feel good switch. It makes it simple to just be at ease and also be more aware. It is impossible to be afraid and yet genuinely smile at the same time. It is a brilliant way to connect with others and in turn ourselves.

- What do I honestly feel happens when I genuinely smile?

- How does it sincerely benefit me?

- How do I feel it can make me more aware?

- How does it really connect me with other people and in turn myself?

- What do I feel it does for my body, mind, and courage?

- How else do I feel that smiling benefits me?

- What do I feel must happen, if sincerely honest for me to smile more?

Paul Fashade B.SC, M.A.

The laughing cure

By Elizabeth Scott, M.S., About.com Guide
Updated: October 07, 2009

Research has shown health benefits of laughter ranging from strengthening the immune system to reducing food cravings to increasing one's threshold for pain. There is even an emerging therapeutic field known as humour therapy to help people heal more quickly, among other things. Humour also has several important stress relieving benefits.

Stress Management Benefits of Laughter:

- Hormones: Laughter reduces the level of stress hormones like cortisol, epinephrine (adrenaline), dopamine and growth hormone. It also increases the level of health-enhancing hormones like endorphins, and neurotransmitters. Laughter increases the number of antibody-producing cells and enhances the effectiveness of T cells. All this means a stronger immune system, as well as fewer physical effects of stress.

- Physical Release: Have you ever felt you "have to laugh or I'll cry"? Have you experienced the cleansed feeling after a good laugh? Laughter provides a physical and emotional release.

- Internal Workout: A good belly laugh exercises the diaphragm, contracts the abs and even works out the shoulders, leaving muscles more relaxed afterward. It even provides a good workout for the heart.

- Distraction: Laughter brings the focus away from anger, guilt, stress, and negative emotions in a more beneficial way than other mere distractions.

- Perspective: Studies show that our response to stressful events can be altered by whether we view something as a 'threat' or a 'challenge'. Humour can give us a more light-hearted perspective and help us view events as 'challenges', thereby making them less threatening and more positive.

- Social Benefits of Laughter: Laughter connects us with others. In addition, laughter is contagious, so if you bring more laughter into your life, you can most likely help others around you to laugh more, and realize these benefits as well. By elevating the mood of those around you, you can reduce their stress levels, and perhaps improve the quality of social interaction you experience with them, reducing your stress level even more!

How to Use Laughter:

Laughter is one of my all-time favourite stress management strategies because it is free, convenient, and beneficial in so many ways. You can get more laughter in your life with the following strategies:

1. T.V. and Movies: There is no shortage of opportunities for laughter from the entertainment industry whether at the theatre, the video store, or at home on the TV. Watching truly hilarious movies and shows is an easy way to get laughter into your life whenever you need it.

2. Laugh with Friends: Going to a movie or comedy club with friends is a great way to get more laughter in your life. The contagious effects of laughter may mean you'll laugh more than you would have done by yourself plus you'll have jokes to reference at later times. Having friends over for a party or game night is also a great setup for laughter and other good feelings.

3. Find Humour In Your Life: Instead of complaining about life's frustrations, try to laugh about them. If something is so frustrating or depressing realise that you can 'look back on it and laugh.' Think of how it will sound as a story you could tell to your friends and then see if you

can laugh about it now. With this attitude, you may also find yourself being more light-hearted and silly, giving yourself and those around you more to laugh about. Approach life in a more mirthful way and you will find you are less stressed about negative events, and you will achieve the health benefits of laughter. (See the article on maintaining a sense of humour listed below).

4. 'Fake It Until You Make It': Just as studies show the positive effects of smiling occur whether the smile is fake or real, faked laughter also provides the benefits mentioned above. So smile more, and fake laughter; you will still achieve positive effects, and the fake merriment may lead to real smiles and laughter.

5. More on Having Fun: See these additional suggestions on laughing more and having fun in your life.

Sources: Bennett MP, Lengacher C. Humour and Laughter May Influence Health: III. Laughter and Health Outcomes. Evidence-Based Complementary and Alternative Medicine, March 2008. Bennett MP, Zeller JM, Rosenberg L, McCann J. The Effect of Mirthful Laughter on Stress and Natural Killer Cell Activity.. Alternative Therapies in Health and Medicine, March-April 2003. Berk LS, Felten DL, Tan SA, Bittman BB, Westengard J. Modulation of Neuroimmne Parameters During the Eustress of Humour-Associated Mirthful Laughter.. Alternative Therapies in Health and Medicine, March 2001. Skinner N, Brewer N. The Dynamics of Threat and Challenge Appraisals Prior to Stressful Achievement Events. Journal of Personality and Social Psychology, September 2002.

4. Your music: "remember to never die with your music or rhythm still in You"

The power of music pulls us in, we feel it, and it takes us to deeper places.

What happens to you when you listen to sounds or music that simply makes you feel great? Do you remember the feeling that builds up in you when you listen to your favourite sounds or music? Create the space in your daily life to listen to sounds that inspire you or simply make you feel good. While you are doing this also visualize your life dreams - it is brilliant for making things happen.

The beauty of mp3 players and i-pods, is that you can multitask, while at the gym or out walking your dogs you can have the pleasure of listening to calming sounds or your favourite music. It makes it much easier to just feel good as often as you wish!

What kinds of sounds and music do you feel move you to do great things?

What music or sounds have inspired you to step into your greater self? List them and make your favourite "play list" and label it, "things that inspire me towards great things" or "to feel brilliant".

It is much better to hypnotise yourself this way than be hypnotised by adverts on the TV to buy something you do not need! This is the beauty of music and sound, we can't see it or touch it… it does not need to be discussed or put into words, we feel it deep down in our cells and hear it in ways words cannot describe.

Do not just turn on your music or sounds, pay attention to your inner guide as you listen to the music and notice what you feel during those best music moments! Build your courage and self-trust so you can genuinely start listening to your heart's rhythm on what to do next…

Music makes you hear the sound of your heart! Act on it!!!

Hear the calling of your heart and do not die before you sing or play your own songs in life or literarily do it… Feel it and get your Courage and self-trust to take you there!

5. The "aaaah" worry-clearing Meditation ("jappa") in just 15 Minutes! It can also be used for manifestation or making things happen...

This is a very effective method to clear one's mind and quickly connect to your body and mind, allowing you to feel inspired. However, you do need a private place to sit with your back straight, head slightly up, facing forward, so you can say the sound "aaah" aloud, parting your lips slightly, and letting the sound radiate up and down your chakra or your meridian points (up and down your power line, your spinal cord to your head), releasing toxins, stressful thoughts and frustrations. It is extremely healing and it lightens your mind load.

This meditation is brilliant for people who have never tried meditation before because they get bored or get frustrated by the mind chatter. Jappa meditation is calming and amazingly effective. You feel strong and aware again. It has an uplifting energy vibration.

Some of these basic methods I have taken from my own regular yoga practice. Don't get caught up in asking yourself why it works – just trust me that it works, experience it and you can always learn the reasons later. The "aaah" meditation is over 2000 years old and the "aaah" sound is in the names of your God depending on your religion whether it is Jehovah, Buddha, Krishna, Mohammed etc. Meditation is free to everyone, you do not need to be religious to practice it. When you start practicing meditation and add manifesting to your practice you will get immediate amazing results that will certainly surprise you. It is particularly good for those that feel they are time constrained.

If you truly want to double the effect - get that wow feeling that gets you refreshed no matter how difficult your mental or physical state, then do the same meditation in the shower. Sit down in the shower; let the water run down your head, back, front, and legs… imagining it washing away all your troubled thoughts. Stay with the "aaah" sound, think of whatever you wish to happen in your life, be it a word or a sentence, pictures etc… and repeat it in your mind while you say your "aaah" sounds. It is truly awakening and calming. Words cannot describe it - it can only be experienced.

What are the benefits? How do you feel it affects your body, mind, courage, and make you feel inspired (remember the literal definition is 'in spirit')?

You can answer this question when you have tried it out first. What do you feel must happen to make this even better for you?

How did you feel afterwards? Please write it down. Remember the incredible feelings that cost you nothing…the well-being, clarity and presence you feel in your moments.

6. Ranting out loud or screaming for 5 minutes non-stop.

… Especially when your pain is unbearable! Forget about your image and your usual rules then you can heal faster and get back to yourself.

… Aim for 5 minutes, it is so effective that you will probably stop in about 3 to 5 minutes or even start laughing. When you have let it all out of your system, you will realise how silly your mind's over dramatisation of it was… I always say crap is better out then in! You will feel light and off load toxic energy and waste quicker.

We need to stop these feelings and reactions before they become rooted in our subconscious. It is much better to stop them dead before they can grow roots in you. This way you will dump any thoughts that do not help you, or that make you react, instead of responding. This will also help stop you getting lost in the mind, yet again.

What else do I feel I can benefit from this?

What else do I feel I can do to make it feel even better?

What must happen for me to know when it is time to do this exercise to get rid of my frustrations, and anxiety?

What else can I do to make myself feel better?

7. Being Right There with the Little Things You Do.

This is a kind of meditation on the little things we do but take for granted. It simply helps us calm down while doing our daily chores e.g. washing a plate and really looking at the foam, and feeling the water run through your fingers, while watching your hand movements on the plate as you wash it. If you can breathe deeply at the same time, you will find yourself to be calmer with your dishes.

Even the daily mundane activities we do that do not need much mental input can become a form of meditation. It is not always necessary to sit down and fold your legs before you meditate! You can meditate taking your bath or shower, cleaning the house, or just be aware of your footsteps as you go up the stairs. Anything that makes you more aware of your moments, bringing you back to yourself will also calm you. It is even better and stronger if you stay conscious with your breathing while doing your chores. In so doing you learn to listen to yourself again and what is really going on. Your self-guide or heart's dialogue will definitely speak louder to you than even before. What you lost along the way will come back to you. It is an incredible sense of presence and power beyond words and you will feel free and damn good just for the hell of it. Now imagine what you can do in that state of body, mind, and courage or spirit, together? Just do it and see. You have nothing to lose, but a hell of a lot to gain, for free!

It will turn your chores into an experience that puts you at ease. You will not need to intentionally make time for meditation. Use your normal chore time as a resource instead and feel what happens - you will be surprised.

8. Do the Little and Big Things You Used to Love, But Forgot, or Just Stopped Doing!

Such as: Short walks, going to your favourite spot that brings you peace and inspires you, enjoying your garden, playing a game, walking your dog, laughing with a friend, calling someone you feel good with that maybe you haven't called for a while... remember to list them all.

What else did you love to do and have stopped doing?

What else have you not done but you sense or know will feel good for sure?

What must happen for you to do the little and big things you used to love to do that made you feel good?

What new things do you feel you must or would love to add to your list if you had the confidence?

List as many as you can, rearrange plans, and then just go do it... Think about what you genuinely have to gain?

9. Help or Care for Someone, Even for a Short While!

There is a very relieving feel good energy that comes to us, like a great gift, when we genuinely help someone else. Even when you pray or send good thoughts to someone else it feels surprisingly good. Sending good energy to others creates harmony and love as a whole. This enables us to come back to our original self — reminding us of our true nature. Money just cannot buy these nice deep feelings!

So, when you help others, you basically help yourself twice as much without realising.

Perhaps we have never really acknowledged the giving of ourselves as important for self nurturing, self growth and feeling good or loved… as this is what happens to the other person when you help them…You literally make a difference to that person and yourself without consciously realising it.

10. The Natural Confidence Warrior's Upright Stand!

Stand straight, back aligned as much as possible, upright with your chest out, and, raising your head up and looking up, then close your eyes, and breathe for a deeper effect! You can also open your eyes if you wish. It is similar to how soldiers stand meditating for hours… yes, the secret is out, they meditate!

Bet you never realised it is a form of meditation. While they stay alert and aware for hours, they can also be both calm and in a warrior state. It is important however to breathe deeply and slowly. This will make one feel strong and grounded immediately, no matter what stressful thoughts you may have. It is very difficult to hold on to any bad feelings or thoughts in this state. Regardless of your thoughts, start with just 5 minutes, just as long as you breathe and keep the physical position you will be in a focused yet calm place.

The more you do it, the more you can get back to your resourceful self quicker. The beauty of this warrior stand is you can do it almost anywhere. No one can tell what you are doing… you could just be looking at the stars, beautiful birds or the clouds, or admiring the trees high up, while you breathe.

And then just ask the question, what must happen from now to just make things better? Your genuine answer will come for that moment. What do I feel I must do from now, to make it better? What else do I feel I can do? List and keep repeating these questions, such as, what else? Your mind will actually help you onwards, as it will respond, not react.

These are very simple and yet powerful positions that make it almost impossible to stay in a non-resourceful low energy state, which will not be much help when we are feeling sad, low, or unhappy. This position, and deep breathing while in it, will shift one in minutes. It is also very useful if you are in a highly stressful job or environment!

11. The Joy of Making Mistakes!

"I have learned more from my mistakes than from my successes."
Sir Humphrey Davy

"We learn wisdom from failure much more than success; we often discover what will do, by finding out what will not do; and probably he who never made a mistake never made a discovery."
Samuel Smiles

"A step in the wrong direction is better than staying on the spot all your life. Once you're moving forward you can correct your course as you go. Your automatic guidance system cannot guide you when you're standing still"
Maxwell Maltz

Some believe we should avoid making mistakes at all costs. As a result our focus becomes based on deep seated fear about making a mistake as opposed to moving with our heart's truth towards what we are for or we choose. Finding our own truth and doing what we feel in our heart is crucial. Know and understand that making a mistake is simply part of our growth. How do you feel you learnt what you clearly know now? If you never had to make any mistakes? If that is the case, what makes us avoid mistakes so much that we end up moving more towards them, unknowingly! The more we think about avoiding the mistake the more we will be drawn to it, instead of thinking towards what we genuinely decide and then just doing it.

We constantly think about the mistake we want to avoid and we will naturally gravitate toward it! Now what would happen if we thought about the mistake but never gave it much charge? Once you acknowledge this…you can just get on with doing and decide on things without fear. It is that simple! So how do you feel about training your mind, and self-talk towards what you actually want to create? What you are for... Rather than what you are against! What do you have to lose?

When we avoid something repeatedly and fearfully in our heads, it is bound to find its way to our doorstep, because at the back of our mind, it is singing loudly, even if we pretend we are avoiding it and so it just shows up. Whatever we think about most of the day will end up showing up. It is just how it is!

So accept the mistakes as they are part of growing and often instrumental in making things turn out better in our lives. I have countless examples of how my mistakes were actually blessings in disguise kicking me into growth. It stopped me from avoiding any situations I did not like, and they turned out to be good for me in the short or long term. This has undoubtedly made my growth and progress in life faster, happier, and in turn, others have benefited by default.

Furthermore, I am not so caught up on whether I get things right or not! It is as if the real result is delayed for a while to grow from the mistake or supposed disaster, and then the real reason or blessing shows itself, sometimes months or years later. Then I smile, and know then why I had to dance with that experience at the time. I realise that it is truly a natural part of evolving, changing, and growing. You will always make mistakes, this is guaranteed! The question is who are you when it happens? And whom do you choose to become in that moment? In the moment after you have stopped being mad or scared, what will you do next to make things better?

It is crucial to speak our truth with love, and understand that it is necessary to make mistakes. Remember that even if you avoid

your mistakes, other people's mistakes will still find you, for your needed growth. It is never about unfairness! The laws of the universe or things that happen to you do not take any notice of human thinking logic - it never works that way. It does what it does and it is never personal. Understand this and, when you stop resisting, you will live life with such ease and create great things, as the universe will conspire for you in the most efficient way possible. Your resistance just causes suffering, it will happen whether you like it or not.

To know that life is always magical, even when it is hell, is pure freedom!

I used to waste so much time trying to think my way out of making a mistake, or simply trying to predict the future, as if anyone can actually fully predict the future! I would convince myself, and then it would never happen as planned, even with all my analysis and intelligent hypothesis. Things happened whether planned or unplanned. The thing is to listen to your genuine heart's truth. Check your thoughts, hear your truth within yourself, and then just do it. If you must plan then remember that planning is at best a good guide, it is never set in stone, no matter how much you think of it.

So, when things do not go according to plan, then do not be disappointed as there might be a better thing coming. We have all had this experience, something that felt like hell 6 months or a year ago is not as bad now. What makes this so? Everything passes, the question is letting go of your past history now! Remember to worry less about your mistake, follow your heart's truth, and get on with creating. You will be surprised at how much you will create and grow in a short period of practising this. The more you do, the better you dance.

Remember that challenges are not an invite for a fight, it is always an invitation to dance with the master...which is you all along, if you practise and learn... that is the surprise!

Like I often remind myself, it is best to develop a backbone rather than a fearful or cowardly wishbone that shadows my true self. What purpose does that serve me? How does it help me? How does avoiding anything help me?

"While one person hesitates because he feels inferior, the other is busy making mistakes and becoming superior." Henry C Link

Two dejected assistants of Thomas Edison said:

"We've just completed our seven hundredth experiment and we still don't have the answer. We have failed."
"No my friends, you haven't failed" replied Mr Edison. *"It's just that we know more about this subject than anyone else alive. And we're closer to finding the answer, because now we know seven hundred things not to do. Don't call it a mistake. Call it an education."*

Just think what we would have lost if Edison had given up because of his many hundred so-called mistakes?! By the way, he made almost ten thousand educational mistakes before discovering the light bulb, for all of us to enjoy! Las Vegas would not exist without Thomas Edison!!

12. Not Living Up to Your Past History Anymore!!

Let me pose a simple question, what would happen if you did not have to live up to your reputation or past history?

What would this mean to your everyday living? And who would you become? Please write or list whatever comes to you, and keep asking, what else? Keep writing, or make an audio recording, until you feel light, and nothing comes anymore. If your mind says I do not know, answer back with…if I did know, under no pressure, what do I feel it could be, if I just guessed?

Everything changes in our body and around us except for the memories we hold on to like children with some sort of soiled diaper. We proudly wear our unhelpful past history; we even choose to be a victim getting some crazy fix from it, like it is our identity! Ironically, this is not what is really happening. People choose to embrace this and become the victim. People walking around with their smelly diapers affect other people taking their energy away. This is usually self-serving, and ugly!

This taking may seem satisfying in the short term but the real price is your soul or spirit always being frozen or stuck in a maze pattern, going round, and around. You also stop yourself receiving your real gifts and growth. It is like you are constantly filling a cup with a hole in it - It will never fill up!

Let us be very aware of what has become to you an unhelpful habit, reputation, or history. It is time to check if it is still true of who you are, or whom you choose to become in your life? If not, decide whom you choose to become from now! Then just start doing.

If your mind says, I do not know, which is the case many times, it is a form of avoidance or the ego saying let me stay in charge. Remember that your ego does not want you to reconnect back to your natural true self. So always remember to say this once again to your mind: 'I know I do not know, but if I did know, what would I guess anyway, no pressure, just guess?'

13. Support and Stepping Up, Especially in Hard Times!

Most people still run away from coaching, support, or guidance. They leave therapy alone because there is still the stigma attached to getting help and some people still believe it means you are emotionally unstable or even psychotic. However the bottom line is, we all need support with our mind injuries. We all need somebody to ask us questions that move us forward beyond our constant blocks and mind spinning that take us away from ourselves into illusionary hell! We cannot do it alone or sometimes get out if we are still inside our head.

You can't solve a problem with the same mind that created it!
Albert Einstein

The thing I like about coaching or alternative therapy is that it moves you forward. Coaching or therapy takes you away from self-victimisation and gets you talking and taking action. Remembering to always ask: **what are you for, rather than against**! We are all very good at stating what we do not like or are against. We always say and do the same things that do not help us rather than stating with the same level of emotion, focus, and frequency, what we are truly and firmly for…or simply towards what helps us. For example, we say, "I hate this person", or "I dislike it when people do"… or "I can't do this or that" and we keep repeating it all the time. We programme ourselves to invite the stranger in us that is against who we truly are, and most of the time, we do not even recognise that is what we are doing.

So enrich your spirit and stay alight and say loudly what you are for, such as "I am for peace and I am for creating this or that", or "I am for enjoying life in this way or that way" and so on. That is what I mean by stating what you are for, so one programmes oneself towards where you heart-fully decide to go. Coaching does not have to come in a form of somebody that you pay. It needs to come in the form of somebody in your life that helps you find your own guide, truth and kicks you into action. I am not talking about **positive thinking (although that's better than nothing)** because positive thinking means that in the back of your mind you still have doubts which is why you are trying so hard to think positively. You are trying to force it. This usually does not work.

Simply ask yourself the questions about what you are for and wait for the answers. Then make it a must by acting on them immediately. Do not delay or find reasons to not do what you know you must. You decide when you take any small action; it is at that point of starting your action that you have truly decided. So having direct quality questions are a must.

When you can engage yourself, through these questions that move and lift you, you get your own direct truth with far less doubt, you are already half way there. When you take action, you are there! It does not matter about failure or whatever you call it. We need to love making mistakes because without making mistakes you do not learn. Furthermore, you simply will not get the big prizes or the big wonderful magical experiences.

Living in the unknown is the key, where you can grow abundantly, and love, creativity, consciousness, and much more shows up. So, get comfortable and enjoy the ride.

To give you an example, remember how you have learnt everything you know so far, including tying your shoes or walking. What would have happened if your parents told you to give up attempting to walk as you kept falling over again and again? Same with all the other things we thought we could not do, but did do to our own surprise. Where would we be today if we gave up on ourselves that easily? This is what I would call "Backbone shrinking" or BS! This is what we physically do. Observe yourself and others when they get afraid or withdraw from something that makes them feel uncomfortable. They shrink their body and their breath becomes shallow.

14. The Joy and Healing Benefits of Touch and Massage!

Massage has amazing healing benefits. This is the one quick fix we all like because it makes us feel good when we are massaged towards healing. It is also unbelievably nurturing. We would not have survived were it not for touch especially when we were babies.

We are virtually the only mammals for which touch is imperative for survival as babies - we could not survive at all without touch or being loved in some way or nurtured, even in the hospital. That is why, as I mentioned previously, premature babies survive at a higher rate when they are held or touched.

During a massage, given with genuine care and love, through

the tension points, we can eliminate our body toxins and receive energy that heals. The massage 'technique' is secondary although still important.

That is why when you sit in a massage chair, it feels good, you enjoy it, and it works. However, it is never going to be the same as when you get a massage and have the physical touch from a professional who genuinely cares, particularly when it is a massage therapist who engages their energy or focus and who will transfer their healing touch.

It is beneficial even if you only manage a massage once a week. Do not wait until you are physically tense, your back is stiff, or you already have pain in your shoulders before you do something. Prevention alongside practical everyday wellness, lightness, and feeling good is crucial. It is always up to you! Do not complain that you are always in pain and irritation – do something about it. Do you wait until your car is messed up before you service it? (Actually, most of us probably do!) Do an "MOT" service on your body. "MOT" in the UK means our car is tested and serviced, it is road worthy to travel and do more mileage safely and can be enjoyed without endangering others and ourselves. We do it yearly by law. We certainly need the same "MOT" for our body meaning at the very least a massage twice a month. It is important that we stop putting a band-aid on our wounds. Instead of taking a pill to reduce the headache, find out what is causing the headache.

Remember that just half an hour of massage once a week, or even 15 minutes on a massage chair is better than nothing. If you really cannot afford a massage then get some DVDs, learn some basic massage techniques to give to your partner or friend and vice versa.

Make sure you get your massage and support from a person or people that actually take care of themselves or from a person that is regularly giving genuine care. You do not want to go to anybody who does not practise what he or she preaches! Then you get the best results. I actively do a complete body and mind detox therapy with my team because the holistic approach is essential to clear out our mind hijacking us. When we release toxins in the body, feel rested, keep hydrated with live water (such as spring or crystallised water), and eat healthy nutritious live food we will feel more alive, and more at ease to create, and do so much more…

From time to time, we can indulge in decadent foods that are not nutritious but taste good. Taste but do not overdo, moderation is key! You are fooling yourself if you believe that you can keep indulging in those types of foods and not put on weight. Excessive eating means that you are not listening to your body, as your body will be saying no, as it cannot clean your body quickly enough – and so you simply expand.

15. Managing Frustrations and Rejections!

"People who fail to achieve their goals usually get stopped by frustration. They allow frustration to keep them from taking the necessary actions that would support them in achieving their desire. You get through this roadblock by ploughing through frustration, taking each setback as feedback you can learn from, and pushing ahead.

I doubt you'll find many successful people who have not experienced this. All successful people learn that success is buried on the other side of frustration. Unfortunately, some people don't get to the other side…The key to success in life is getting and handling massive frustrations"
Anthony Robbins

Embrace your frustrations and look at them as healthy challenges that will build your backbone and creativity. Turn frustrations into something fascinating in your mind's thinking. Try making it smaller in your mind or changing the volume on what you say to yourself and how you say it; change the colour, change your physical state or what you do with your body - remember extend rather than shrink.

There will be times when you will experience rejection from family, friends, or your 'tribe'. As your circumstances begin to change for the better, your friends may change as well. Not everyone will be celebrating the changes they see in you even when it is for the better. There is a lot of truth in the old saying 'misery loves company'! Your 'tribe' will generally want you to stay the same - it's not within 'tribe rules' to grow, become increasingly independent let alone leave to genuinely find your own path, even if you've learnt everything that your tribe could teach you. But you will definitely build your backbone as you move forward with your truth. Just try to bear in mind, without blame, judgement, or analysis that your tribe will want to keep you still – after all, we all do silly things out of fear or a sense of loss!

It is true that it is still the minority of people who can genuinely handle frustration and rejection. But when you learn to handle these two things there is honestly very little that can stop you in our mind-thinking world. Remember that 'mind-thinking' is limited anyway so never let it be your only personal standard or only point of referencing, then you will always have an advantage.

"The way you activate the seeds of your creation is by making choices about the results you want to create. When you make a choice, you mobilise vast human energies and resources which otherwise go untapped. All too often people fail to focus their choices upon results and therefore their choices are ineffective. If you limit your choices only to what seems possible or reasonable, you disconnect yourself from what you truly want, and all that is left is compromise."
Robert Fritz

CHAPTER 6

HEART-FULLY, HAPPY AND CONTENT NOW, REGARDLESS!

Well, we have now talked about several things like standing upright, the importance of breath and motion, receiving a massage and receiving coaching and guidance. Remember that about 90% of the things we worry about rarely happen yet we spend so many hours stuck on a problem. Sometimes we can even spend months stewing on the problem. Indeed, some stew on it forever because we get a lot of attention from others and ourselves when we play the victim. We exchange our sense victimisation with others… 'Look at me; my problem is bigger than yours; my day is worse than yours; O God why is this happening to me' etc…

We falsely believe we are getting love from playing the victim, but it is a sad, low energy state. You will have a horrible feeling deep down, feel like you are never enough, you will be a shadow of a person. We never really believe in the love given to us in that state, we cannot deeply buy into it as we receive it while not being our genuine self. You will always want constant refills to feed the victim self. Remember that the suffering will never really go away for you and you are forcing other people to play along through the back door.

We keep feeding the fire with even more petrol and it keeps burning and eating us alive. This fixated victim becomes addicted to this way of thinking because he or she thrives on the attention and as long as there is someone around to listen, he/she gets the fix they crave. However, in the long run, the side effects are damaging to their body and mind. They are never free from constantly wanting approval from others. They never feel worthy enough. They probably do not know any other way to really connect or get love. It is very hard to try to come to terms with and stop playing the victim. Most people stay in this state until they die, swinging in and out but without ever stepping into who they really are. They become a stranger to themselves. They do not have the self-truth or real courage to do anything heartfelt or to speak their genuine truth.

We literally do anything to connect and to get love. This is because it is something we used to get for free. When we were babies we would be loved even when we peed in our pants! Then comes the time when we are deemed more grown up to fit in, and follow the rules usually unconsciously. Then it all becomes about performance! We have to tell good stories, or perform in some way to get love or attention most of the time. This required more effort on our part and it also drained energy from us. This is how we start to condition ourselves to have all these habits, all these short-lived, unhelpful habits to get attention or love.

This part of the book is about the practical things we can do to learn better habits. Better habits that are easily sustainable for our everyday living and lifestyle and will actually help us naturally without falseness. There are many brilliant personal development courses out there and they have some fantastic materials for developing but they do not tell you or guide you directly on the basic things. They do not tell you clearly where you need to be to even start or have a chance to stay with it and move forward without slipping - you know what I mean!

The basic thing that you can easily do is to practice grounding yourself. You must have this foundation before you can get into the habit of learning without going backwards. The basic things are so simple yet absolutely vital and must be done! One has got to be grounded to even learn let alone start applying most of the material that's out there otherwise it will become just another interesting read, just another fascinating audio recording that resonates with us somewhere but we don't know what to do with it. Or we talk about it for a little while or we do something with it for a little while and then it fades away into the background. We get distracted again, doing more and more 'stuff' - you know work, paper work/bills, accounting, shopping or getting stuck with some other problem. It was interesting at the time but now has gone. Why? Because our grounding is weak. Our table needs four legs but it only has two or three, so our table collapses when we put any small load on it. It will never stay upright for long. We have to get the basics right. The basics are the practical things that take no time. We should be well conditioned to do these practical things as when you have them awakened in you every thing that you want to learn, you want to do, you want to create, you want to make happen or you want to solve will all become possible! However, if you do not get these basic things wired in, forget it! It is like having no foundation to your home and it is only a matter of time before your home crumbles. When we are not grounded, we spin around the same maze and never complete a desired outcome. Look at your foundation. Does it have cracks in it? If so, go back to the basics and build that foundation up from the ground.

These basic things do not require much time. Make them a new habit. Then we can begin meeting our challenges and moving toward our desires and creativity. If we do not do these things, it is like climbing up Mount Everest barefoot! You are trying to do things the hard way. What is the benefit of doing that exactly?

We can very easily build our foundation by starting to practice asking ourselves some simple questions. Make it an everyday habit like brushing your teeth or going to the toilet or cleaning yourself. I am not being sarcastic here but for crying out loud, it is not that much of a big deal, we need to just do it, when we are ready…

Once we can do what will get us back to ourselves faster, and when we are back, only then are we the captain of our own ship. This means everything working with us as part of a team; our mind and our heart working with us and our body working with us. We then have a natural synchronisation, which our body ("buddy") does anyway. Our cells function, they communicate with each other, they know the best things to do for us, they know what to do with the food we eat, they know what quantity of energy we require to do a certain action, they do all these things, communicating intelligently without us doing much! Our body breathes for us, we do not breathe for our body. We restrict our breath when we think, shrink, and worry. This is why our "buddy" forces us to yawn or take a deep breath. So we need to do these basic things for ourselves otherwise it will remain challenging for us. Remember that externalities will try to influence us to pull away from these basic things; externalities move us away from ourselves, externalities make us become a stranger to who we are if we rely on them excessively to guide us.

Most people do not even recognise who the hell they are; that is why they are consistently unhappy, swinging in and out with fear based thoughts. They are miserable because they do not have the basic skills to get them back to themselves. How can we recognise who we are or try to make decisions for ourselves when we are dealing with a stranger's performance while running an illusion? Can you see how ridiculous the whole show is? Then we wonder why we cannot do anything, or get much working for us, why our life is not flowing forward, including our relationships. How can we have a relationship if we are not our true self and yet still expect the relationship to work?

So we must get the basic stuff grounded, like conscious breathing, especially when it matters! And we try whining or blaming somebody else but the bottom line is we are not self aware, nor

ready to see the basic things that truly make us resourceful and genuinely useful to others and ourselves.

I want us to talk about the things that we can do that will still wake us up to our higher frequency including the higher spiritual side. They must be very practical and once we get into the helpful habits and are awake, we are more than half way there. We do not have to use fancy words or phrases to be doing it and to be getting the full benefit. Let us start with the basics. For example, when going up any stairs, we can meditate. What do I mean by that? Well, just breathe and actually be conscious of each step you are taking up the stairs. When you breathe deeply (rather than shallow) you will become calm, you will become aware, you will start teaching yourself to be in the moment… that is meditation. It also creates a certain inner calmness along with a natural healing process that will vibrate throughout your body. When you walk up and down the stairs and if you are deep breathing at the same time, you will find that your mind is calmer and clearer. You are in the moment and your focus is not so much on the task as it is on the breath.

Another example, one that smokers will identify with - although I definitely do not advocate the smoking part - is when you go out for a cigarette. You step out into the sun, you light up the cigarette, you take a deep breath - in a way that is a kind of a meditation. You are in a really powerful state of self-connection.

Smoking meditation is not the kind of thing I am advocating here, we want to focus on the things that do not physically or mentally hurt us. Let me make that emphatically clear! I am talking about moving while breathing deeper. Go for a walk or even when you are just walking back from work, breathe deeply and you will become aware of the trees or simply more aware of what's actually going on around you.

When you have done some of that, you will feel good, you will come back to work or simply be yourself, whatever you are doing, you will feel refreshed, you are ready to go for another couple of hours or more. People sometimes call it daydreaming, but it is not, it is meditation, as you are aware of your environment and your breathing. Daydreaming is purely in the head, running a sideshow, or webbing pictures movies and sounds that do not help us.

One could also be in a bath with nice candles and oils, listening to calming music, taking deep breaths and feeling the steam all around, enjoying the relaxation and the calmness of the bath. This is also meditation. Set up a section of your home for pure relaxation minus any 'addictive' treats. The relaxation harmonises you and your body will respond and heal itself, like it breathes for you already. Your "buddy" will take any possible chance to make you feel good, it will take any chance to heal you.

When you fall sick, are blowing your nose, shivering, and sweating, you are not really sick. You are just cleansing because there are lots of toxins stored in your body that your "buddy" has not had the time to sort out. You have been demanding energy from your body, overloading it, causing your body to become depleted. Remember, your "buddy" has to get rid of anything it cannot use. If it cannot lose it, because it is too busy giving you energy to do things, or is constantly fire fighting all the toxins we keep putting in (like alcohol, like caffeine, like eating too late for proper digestion, like eating too much acidic-based food like meat) we will eventually get sick.

I am not saying you should not eat all these tasty things, but here is the thing, you also need to have alkaline-based foods to actually break down all the acid you are putting in. If you do not do that, then you are just piling on more and more crap and expecting your "buddy" to quickly sort it out. Who or what else is going to sort it out? Do we think some fairy godmother is going to come down from the sky and clear out all the crap in our body? Our "buddy" is going to have to sort it all out, because we are not going to do it! But at some point, we all have to help our body, because without our "buddy" we cannot live nor feel good.

We are the one who started it. We are the one who caused it. It did not just happen by accident. Please let us get real, and be honest here! I know nobody wants to hear this but it is not about blame, it is just what happens constantly. The question is, do you want to eat just to fill up or do you want to actually help yourself physically and mentally? If you want to eat to enjoy and to gain energy and feel good, while regenerating, then eat more live food and juice. Have you noticed that some foods are just so tasteless when we eat them? These genetically modified foods taste so boring and lifeless! Real organic food is alive and tasty! I know it can be a little bit more expensive, but aren't we worth spending money on? When our body gives up, we eventually have to go to the doctor or take some medicine it will certainly cost us more then. You will also spend loads of time recovering, for sure.

It is time to get familiar and consciously take care of you. Even an ostrich does not bury his head in the sand for too long!! We have got to get our basics right and wake up our courage. However, it is hard to hear ourselves when we do not feel good. It becomes harder and harder to get back to a healthy state without help from someone else i.e. doctors, homeopaths, healers.

If, however, we consciously take some basic time for ourselves, eat tasty food, and nutrients to feel good, and do more, then your heart and "buddy" will harmonise with your thoughts, and then your mind will become a team player with your heart's truth.

On holiday with the mind

When we meditate, we can go anywhere. Our mind is a very powerful tool; it is not just for thinking! I do not feel or think that we have even thought about what our mind does, or what it is actually capable of doing. We have not even got that far yet. We just get up every day and think of the same old things. We do the same practical things; we do not teach or go further with our minds to do all the other interesting, gifted things it has waiting for us. Do you realise, that you can re-live, enjoy, and revive the same physical feelings you get from going on your many holidays on a daily basis.

At my workshops and my coaching sessions, we engage all the normal senses, which is the visual, taste, touch, feel, smell, hearing and the 'x factor'. The x factor is what moves you into your zone and makes your spirit alight. You feel driven by something but not sure what. It is a euphoric feeling. It is like all your cells are singing in harmony. The words are irrelevant, what it feels and means to us is what counts. Our mind is a very powerful tool and resource to us; it has the ability to visualise in ways that can affect us physically and immediately!

Imagine closing your eyes, and in your mind's eye go to the place where you had your best ever holiday, where you felt so good, in your own special place. Take a deep breath, stay with your breathing while you think about this special place of yours. See yourself there again. Smell what you smelt there, taste what you tasted there, hear what you heard there, feel deeply what you sensed there, and breathe it in deeply in your mind's eye in your special place and be there again, with your heart fully open, loving it.

All you need to do is simply close your eyes, it could be anywhere on the tubes or trains - you can visualise exactly being there in your special place. Then you breathe it in even more…you breathe in even more to enjoy it. Now what else can you do, you can double the emotions of being there, even triple it while you take an even deeper breath. You will see and hear the sounds of the sea, or your favourite view, in your own special place.

It is what I call the true songs of your holiday, the forgotten notes that you can replay anytime you choose. It is your own special meditation, your own signature, and a call back to yourself, your zone to do even greater things.

Remember this, every time you are lost with your stranger and you want to feel good again, you can redesign that special place the way you want. You will see what inspires, and moves you in your special place. Hear and feel what touches the depths of your being, feel the amazing sensations, taste whatever tantalises your taste buds, smell the best aromas that stir your senses beyond words. You will feel calm; take deep breaths in while you close your eyes. It does not matter where you are; when you do this practiced breathing you will double the emotions where you are, or even triple it. You will definitely get the feeling of being back on holiday again, because your mind remembers and your heart stimulates the rest. **Your heart remembers how you felt, it remembers why it was so special to you, regardless of what you thought, your heart knows you best and, unlike your mind, it doesn't doubt**!

All you have to do is visit your brilliant memories more frequently and then add more memories to them, make them more amazing through your mind's eye. That is all you have to do. It takes less than a minute to go there as it takes less time when you journey with your mind.

Now remember when you pay for a holiday, you make the effort to travel to the airport; you check in, go through all the security, go through all the queues, you wait in the lobby to board, you hang around until you are bored, trying to amuse yourself, and all the while, you just want to get on with it and fly. You even buy more stuff, stuff you do not really need while hanging around for the plane. Then you finally fly. You finally get to your destination and land. You then have to transfer to your hotel or accommodation, and you have to check in again. Before you even start your holiday, you have spent hours upon hours in transport! That is a lot of time, money, energy, and your life invested in your holiday.

Now, why wouldn't you want to you use this memory, that has taken some much effort to experience? Why wouldn't we want to use it again and again, to self heal, and feel refreshed? We have been told by all the marketing agents, TV, press, that you can only experience all these feelings on the holiday so we pay to do it again and again but why wait until then? Do we feel we must pay again to go there and feel the same things again? Who said this, who told us that this is the only way?

It is like we have bought a brand new beautiful car of our dreams and then only drive it once or only on special occasions. It is like buying a beautiful dress or suit that makes us feel amazing, that we have worked so hard to pay for, and then only wearing it once. What makes this so, do we even ask? Who told us that is how we must do it? It is just sitting there in the closet waiting for you to put it on and feel good. It does not always need to be worn somewhere special, does it?

Or to give you another example, it's like going to a beautiful restaurant with great food, we pay for the food, it's sitting on our table, we can smell it's wonderful aroma but then we eat it fast, probably talking while eating, so we never really enjoy the food. We probably never really played with the amazing taste in our mouth, really savouring the food so we can relive the experience again. Why not? Enjoy every taste, especially if it is good. We have all been there. It is like when we are at ease, relaxed just after an orgasm, that blissful moment when we quiet down our minds, and feel so content, present, and undisturbed by anything. This is probably the only form of meditation or sincere natural calm some people get!

Try and remember at least 100 experiences or memories from your holidays or life events. I am sure when you've finished, not only will you walk down memory lane, you will feel as if you were there yet again and will certainly feel happy!

We simply do not think about our good memories, let alone great ones nor write them down. It is not a taboo. It is just that we tend to ride on a negative wave. Our unhelpful thoughts overcrowd and drown out our great memories. However, we need to use these helpful thoughts, and memories, as they are such a great gift. What is stopping you from using your mind for your own benefit? Remember, if you do not stimulate your mind, and heart, your mind simply gets bored. If we are not doing something purposeful, or stimulating, nor that we truly love it is inevitable we will get bored. And when we get bored, our worry mind with our stranger simply takes over again. It will find something to do, because it is bored. We stay conditioned towards fear and worse still, we help it along and harden it even further. We become an old dog that virtually cannot be taught new tricks, especially by ourselves, let alone others.

Your mind will go to where it can most easily drift. Our minds are not trained or conditioned to be led by us, nor are most of us able to observe our thoughts and decide what is genuinely true for us and what is not. Instead, our minds lead us using our weaknesses, irritations, and fears.

Do you ever observe your thoughts to see if they are true? Are you asleep, or genuinely awake, if you are sincerely honest? Much of the time we are walking around doing what we do automatically and robotically without any deep feeling or love for it.

When this is happening, we are not present, we are gone, and our body is in turmoil. We are not feeling great, we are not enjoying what is at hand, and we are just ticking along and honestly dead bored! We are constantly spinning webs in our head with unhelpful thoughts and analysis. It is truly a kind of madness in silence. We get stuck in a nightmare that never ends. Our personal power is foreign to us and we lack courage to bring it back. But, is it true to say we are unable to awaken our personal power? We all have a choice to stay where we are, until we choose not to be there. We just have to choose when we have had enough.

We must never forget that we must be the boss of ourselves - not our ego mind and unhelpful thoughts! So, whatever we do, we must get into the habit of steering, or driving our mind where we choose for it to go, so it helps us. The alternative is truly madness, disguised as civilised logical thinking! We are strong enough to make the changes in ourselves, especially if we truly want to be our own experts, and get to listen to our true voice. We are just not consciously aware of it, and have not trained ourselves to do it automatically. We must reprioritise, stressing and acknowledging the importance of those practical tools that will get us there since we genuinely now know what "not doing it" means to us!

When we are able to hear our heartfelt truth, we will create abundance in most part of our lives. Abundance will flow naturally, because you are open to giving and receiving from your heart's truth. Engaging all our senses again, to come back home more frequently, must be our number one priority. Everything else will then fall into place even our biggest problems or challenges.

Our mind is amazing. Past experiences, all that information is filed in our mind like a library full of great books and great memories, yet we do not re-read, or re-visit, let alone apply all that knowledge.

For example, we say we have learnt from our previous heartbreaks, our past relationships, but have we? Do we revisit our past wounds? Do we ask what went wrong and what we could have done to make it better? We may even have listened to audiotapes or read books but in effect we have just filed it in our heads. However, when it comes to applying this new knowledge we fall back on our past triggers that have nothing to do with that new moment or what is now being discussed. Instead, we vent our anger and irritation, usually blaming the other person. **One wonders how many people are really in the same relationship each time! It seems as if there is an entourage of pain connected with people we have collected from our past, such as parents, ex-girlfriends, ex-boyfriends etc. When the cloud has settled, if there is genuine love there, it is realised. However, if there is no real depth or love, they soon part with both parties' ego trapped about being right or wrong.**

Remember that if you use your helpful memories and read the great books in your mind's library, including all the great things that you have done that have clearly brought you back to yourself, they can be useful tools for the present moment. Remember, our foundation needs to be grounded, if not, we will simply crumble and we will fall.

One of the things we are now going to talk about is asking powerful questions that shift us forward with far less doubt. You need to practise with family and friends. Knowing how the mind responds to what is being said or to questions asked is a very powerful and important tool. Your mind does not understand positive or negative, it just responds to whatever is said or to instructions given.

Imagine the fact that we do not really talk to people in the physical sense. Instead, we are always addressing their existing movies, pictures and sounds running in their minds! How would that affect how you communicate with others, let alone yourself?

CHAPTER 7

THE BIG "WHY" TALE…AND EVEN MORE INSPIRING QUESTIONS…

Now let us talk about the word Why – a word that usually triggers a tale or story. When I was a kid and I asked my mother: 'Why is this, why is that?' My mother would say to me, 'because "Why" has a long tail…and a tale for it!' It used to confuse the hell out of me but it always got me quiet, trying to figure it out and of course, my questions would stop, and my mum would have peace again for a while.

Metaphorically, my mum was saying "Why" always has a long story. "Why" questions, by my own extensive experience, always create a negative stomach nudging reaction, no matter your nationality. I know it is not the best way to start asking questions of yourself or of other people. Absolutely not! It stimulates the story part of us, it stimulates the defensive hence the lying element from people. It stimulates the illusionary part of people; it stimulates all the parts of people that are mostly reactive and fear based.

When you ask a Why question most people get a little uptight, have a little clench in their stomach, or start putting on their armour.

Nobody thinks 'oh yeah a why question, I really like that, let me respond!' Now what makes this so? I have realised a very important thing - we have to create stories once the Why question is asked. What makes this pattern so? When we were infants, our parents or guardians loved us unequivocally even if we were sometimes too young to understand it. Once we got older and deemed old enough to know better, we then had to create stories, or give a performance, to receive love like we use to, making a connection and wanting to simply satisfy our parents for love and to be acknowledged as being enough.

We all act out the performance of the "why" tale when something happens, we all do it, no matter your background. For example, think back to when you were young, you break something, you know your parents are coming home and you are old enough to know that you are going to be in trouble, you know what questions will be coming… 'Why did you do this…why did you do that?'

Now, what did you say or how did you react to those why questions? You started to recreate your own tale. Even before your parents got home, you get ready. You run the story in your head, even if you have chosen to tell the truth, you will still try to gloss it nicely so it is presented in a way that minimises the punishment you could get. Therefore, what you learnt was to come up with a good story in response to being asked why in order to minimise or avoid punishment. So, since we were very little, this habit or behaviour has been wired into our subconscious mind.

Here is the funny thing, when people ask you "Why" questions, they have usually already decided what the answer is or should be. Before they ask you the "Why" question they have probably already judged and analysed you. It is a highly evolved person who is able to wait until they hear your truth first. Can you remember when you have asked a "Why" question and you were fully satisfied with somebody's answer? It is a rare thing if one has already prejudged unintentionally or unconsciously.

So when somebody asks you a "Why" question, some suggestions are: 'Could you please tell me what you think the answer is and then we can start from there. I can see you are really upset?'

It does depend on who you are talking to, if it is a friend you can simply say: 'I believe and I sense that you have thought about this and you have a reason in your mind already before you asked me the question.' And maybe he or she will say: 'I thought you did it because of...' You then say that part may be correct and this bit not, and then you adjust. But the person asking the question gets to have their say first, as they are upset, and they must clear out or vent before you can start. Otherwise, they will not really listen to your truth. By doing this, you will know where they are coming from to have a better resolve – especially now knowing they will already have a story on their mind. However, if you are trying to explain the why, you will rarely get a genuine resolution.

Here is another important point - when you ask "Why" questions, people react, it gets their back up, it gets them irritable, even if they don't show it, it rarely creates a connection, or makes love grow. "Why" questions do not create a connection. "Why" questions usually mean you are guilty and need to explain yourself! "Why" questions make most people feel judged, they make you feel like you are in court. They make you feel like you have done something wrong, and feel like a kid again, and you have got to come up with a good tale or justification.

There is hardly anyone who enjoys being asked Why questions. It is most likely that you will not receive the genuine truth if you ask the question "Why". Instead ask questions, that create a response, not a reaction, or disconnection, such as: What has actually happened, please tell me your genuine truth?

- What genuinely made you do…?
- What do you feel made you do…?
- How did this honestly come about?
- What does that mean to you?

- What do you feel about what just happened?
- What do you feel is your genuine reason for doing this?

- *Not, Could you please explain why you did this? No…!*

More questions:

- What truly happened and how can you genuinely make it better?
- What made this happen and how do you feel you can make it better?
- How did this come about and how can you start to make it better from now?

When you use what or how at the start of your questions you will see, that it does not invoke irritation or tightness in the stomach, nor does it invoke anger, and it is not passive either. It will most likely get you closer to the genuine truth. In addition, it will create a response in most cases, without the friction, as people do not feel they are being scrutinised or ambushed. So, you have to ask better questions. Questions that pave the way to moving forward. Ask Questions that inspire creativity, questions that inspire the truth. One will get more of the truth, you will get more clarity, and you will get quicker resolution this way with less friction.

More suggested better questions…

- What do I feel I must do to make this work better?
- What can I do to learn about this or that…?
- What must happen for me to make this better?
- What must genuinely happen for me to actually improve on this or that…?
- What do I feel I must do differently from now about this if dead honest…?

My favourite ones are:

- If I had the courage, what do I feel I would do differently?
- If I had the backbone, what do I feel I will do from now?

Be Surprised

- If I had confidence, what do I feel I would do differently about this from now on?
- If I had confidence, what must I do to make this better from now on?

All these questions will trigger off your brain and automatically move you into a forward looking doing mode. So, if you ask the question, you will get the answer. It is best to give yourself the permission to play, with your own mind, and your inner guide. Now, if your brain says: "I don't know", say to yourself, or ask somebody to ask you these questions:

If you had the courage, what must you do?

If you had the confidence to change the situation, what do you really feel must happen now?

Alternatively, what must you do differently, if you had the confidence to adapt to the situation?

Or what must you do differently, if you had confidence to make it better from now?

If your brain still says I do not know then remember you have got to say firmly: "I know, I don't know, but if I simply guessed, under no pressure, what would it be?" And then wait for it, the genuine you will respond. Just keep repeating the same questions, you may need to be a little patient, and the clarity will come. If you and your inner guide respond with something, such as: "Maybe I could do this and that. I can do that now to just make it better." Ask further: "Well, when exactly must I do this?"

You see, from nothing ("no thing") something will come. Suddenly from being a victim comes resolve. These questions work all the time, yes, all the time. They will always trigger something helpful and give a surprising genuine resolve.

When you ask a question that kicks you into the moment, you begin to breathe. That is the only way you can get creative with completely new ideas. Deep breathing is vital if you want to be creative and come up with something new. You will naturally also tap into your relevant past references, your instinct, what's going on around you, what's going on in your head, what's going on in the real world in that moment… remember to breathe. Guessing allows you to be creative without the pressure… giving yourself the permission to come up with ideas without the analysis or hard push, which usually shuts down creativity! These questions will stimulate you to move in the right direction. It is absolutely vital to ask yourself the questions that truly help you. It works! If it does not, then go back to your "Why" questions if you still believe that will truly help you. But if you want to step up and get bold, ask questions:

If I had the backbone, with genuine confidence, what would I do differently from now?

The moment you do something is the time you decide! Your action decides on something immediately! I have practised and experienced asking genuine questions with many people, including my clients, and they have received amazing results. No analysis. No delays. If you just respond and hear what is coming from your genuine self and then take action, that is all that's required. If one practises it, teaches it, or just speaks about it to somebody else, your attitude about it will be different, you will learn it better, and your quality of life and health will improve. Find out your own genuine truth without fear or without ego in the way. If it is true for you then talk about it with somebody else, talk because when you are teaching it, you have a whole different attitude to it. You make it your own and it becomes a practice for you. It will stay with you and will get rooted. You then develop strong legs to hold up your table creating a firmer foundation. You will get more familiar with what feels good and what works for you. This will help build your own courage and self-trust with far less doubt!

These are the secrets we should have been told and learnt at school and from our parents. This is what makes some people highly successful as they were guided to trust themselves. They practise doing their heart-full courageous thoughts and ideas without question - they step into action. Courage and self-trust stimulates your true gifts to come out when you are truly ready for it. It has always been in you. It is time to wake up, go and do our best, with your heart fully open and your eyes aware! Then you will blossom and do what you are meant to do. Remember you will always adapt and find a resolve on challenges like you have always done. It gets easier as you listen more deeply to yourself, so this must never be the excuse or fear against just starting.

CHAPTER 8

THE MAIN KEY "KI" TO OPEN OUR SENSES…

What practical things can you do to get back to one's genuine self? We have looked at some of the different ways we know from sitting upright, deep breathing, and connecting with our other senses. By getting back to being more aware of ourselves, we do less unhelpful thinking and can more easily get on with what is at hand. When we consciously breathe, we engage all our senses, we engage our thinking, and they both join the team for genuine action. When we just think, without conscious breathing, it is usually an isolated approach. When we are more aware of our breathing and we are engaged by breathing deeply and consciously, this in turn engages our key - "ki" "kinaesthetic internal" (which means what you feel inside), which in turn switches on our other senses.

We are more than just our thoughts; our body is our vehicle for experiencing and doing great things. When we are more aware of our thoughts and feelings, this means that we can access ourselves more easily and frequently and take our true genuine action. This happens authentically and with ease through our hearts.

Straighten Up To Fly...

We truly have to start with practical things, such as deep breathing, yoga and posturing that will help us to get back to ourselves more quickly. Then it will start to become more of a pleasure, as you repeat it more frequently it will become a better habit and finally it will get more enjoyable. You will feel immense pleasure, inner calm and natural confidence from actually doing these little things, which can be achieved within seconds or minutes.

If you really want something to materialise then by setting your intention for it as you breathe deeply is one sure way it will quickly happen. You connect to self from the breathing and your thoughts become focused on what you want to see happen in your life. Once you have practiced the deep breathing, you will notice an enhanced change in clarity and energy, leaving you feeling refreshed, at ease and motivated.

Yoga is a form of exercise for the mind, body, and spirit. When engaged in yoga, one can more easily quieten the mind noise and webbing through breathing and challenging postures. On many occasions as you practise yoga as you breath and focus the body on certain postures you can receive clarity or visions on what to do next.

Different body postures can change your energy state. For example, when you are standing upright with your chin up, you are in peak position. In this upright position, it is difficult to be down and have low energy. Equally, if one is slouched over with your shoulders forward, it is impossible to have a high-energy state. In this position, the body is restricted and deep breaths and energy cannot flow.

This means we limit ourselves physically and in breath and in so doing we promote our sense of lack and limitations as we unknowingly condition ourselves in this way!

When you are aware that you are thinking unhelpful thoughts, try and be conscious of your breathing and posture and make a physical shift outwards often and you will notice a shift in thought as well. One way to get back to your self is to focus on standing upright, chest out and chin up and focus on deep breathing, it's a form of meditation.

Simply, stand or walk upright, chest out, chin up breathing deeply from your stomach/chest area…even if you try to think about what makes you depressed or makes you feel down, you will find that it is very hard to stay there. This is because your body will be more engaged with your senses, making it harder to get into one's drama or illusions (mind webbing). The real you will slowly emerge because your body, cells, natural intelligence plus your natural state of being will not allow you to get repeatedly sucked back into unhelpful thought patterns. As you become more present, as you are breathing consciously, with better physiology and motion, it will mean you won't revert back to those negative patterns of unhelpful conditioning as often. When we breathe in and out fully, we feel more…we simply go to our truth more… leading us to our self-truth and courage to then create what our heart truly desires without slipping!

These daily "must do" checks on our physiology, or what we are doing with our body, will reduce the mind spinning and, as a result, we will not stay with unhelpful thoughts long enough for them to harm us. We will be strengthening our muscles for natural self-healing and self-awareness. All you need to do is just practice them, just do them and you will see the benefit. It is not rocket science as one of my close friends frequently likes to say! Do not just do this when you are feeling down, but make it apart of your lifestyle when you go for a walk, or eat with your family, or talk with friends. Also, avoid doing this if you are smoking, or doing any other addictive activities. You do not want to create a strong anchoring while engaged in addictive activities as you will just be anchoring to your false self and this will make quitting that activity even harder!

Is Your Mind a Foe or a Friend?

The more you are thinking…the less you are breathing! Observe yourself and others if you do not believe me! We are not supposed to be thinking for long. The mind is designed for making quick decisions. This is what makes it so essential that you are aware and breathe more consciously, so your system, with all your senses can reach peak performance. You heart and natural state will be aligned and this will lead "your self team" (body, mind, and inner guide or spirit) to be able to access what you need, including only what is relevant in your mind in your moments to decide! The mind will not go into excessive analysis when you consciously deep breathe. All that comes to you is just what is needed and relevant. The mind will not waste energy holding us back or delaying the process.

When the body perceives a crisis your whole system becomes engaged; your senses, your instinct, your heart, your lungs, whatever is going on right in that moment, 'fight or flight mode'. Your mind and senses becomes acutely aware of what to do, you get into knowing or self-trust survival mode, which in turn makes you naturally courageous, even when you are totally afraid.

Your brain can only do two things, it can hold on to what you put in the present moment (which quickly becomes past data), and it can project past data into the future (your imagination). It takes in what is going on now hence you need to be in the moment to be fully aware of new experiences!

> **So when you access your brain you are accessing your past data and then you are imaginatively projecting it into the future. As we are just referencing past data in our minds this usually takes us towards fear… so it must never be your only source of reference for you or anyone.**

You have to trust your whole natural system more as this is where your real self waits to be given permission to surface. This is where you will get your truth, courage, and self-trust! It is that simple if you choose to play there. The beauty of the way our system is that the mind constantly communicates with your cells, muscles, and your organs etc. Your system does everything automatically without much help from you, even breathing.

When we directly go to thinking, we give away our power as we allow our thinking to take charge of our body, ignore our spirit, leaving our self-truth and trust to take second place and we become our own shadow yet again. What makes this so? Who do we become when we go there? When our bodies are under stress, especially when we hold our breath, we think more towards our fears.

These things I am saying to you are our absolute keys ("ki" turns you on, back to your genuine self-trust, less doubt and then courage to create or make happen what you feel you must or are truly ready for…!). So if you are really ready and want to get the benefit of efficient thinking and running of your system, including wellness of the body and mind then start with your key ("ki") and practise doing these basic things, such as Breathing, Motion, Posture, and Drinking live water, so you get aware just for you.

Conscious breathing in your moments before you yawn.

Let your creativity play, as often as possible, from being in the moment through conscious breathing! Most individuals that create an original idea find that it has come from an inspiring place. Breathing can also bring you back to yourself. Sometimes, when you find yourself thinking so much your body actually forces you to yawn, so you breathe, as you have forgotten to do so! It means you have been restricting your breath for too long, and your breath is needed for all the demands you are placing on your body, hence your intelligent "buddy," literally makes you take a bigger breath (yawning) to stop you getting tired from lack of air or breathing!

Crucial Recap

The more you breathe the more creative you will become and the more you can come up with something original. The more you feel wellness the more you kick into what is relevant in that moment rather than spinning off, analysing and worrying about things that most of the time rarely happen anyway.

So again, I am emphasising this very important element of breath! Why, because breathing is not what most of us do, right, we don't do breathing, we restrict breathing! But breathing happens automatically! If you want to test this theory, try holding your breath and see how long your body will allow you to do that... It is your body that wants to keep you alive!

It wants to keep you alive, hence, you breathe automatically. When we worry, we shrink and we close in. However, when we are happy we extend and spread out, we take in more air, we fill up, we feel invigorated. What does this mean to us?

We know our body is virtually 70-80% water and it needs lots of fresh air and water. It needs these two things. When you do not have enough fresh air to breathe in, or consume enough clean water, your cells will die faster and the ageing process will also speed up. Everybody knows they need to regularly drink live water, but bizarrely nobody regularly talks about breathing, which I find very odd! These are two huge things guaranteed to make you feel good, healthy, plus get back to your real self. When your body is in a healthy state, it makes it easier for the mind to have more peace, more clarity, and more awareness to be and live more fully. Taking care of your body and mind grounds self-trust and courage.

All these things that make you feel good are completely logical. They are the key to your natural, peaceful mind state. It is the best state to be in, it makes you stronger, you are clearer, you are calmer, you also feel more assertive but without any friction. It is effortless, like everything else in the universe, like the trees that withstand harsh weather conditions and still stand effortlessly dancing in the wind. Like the birds in the sky that fly in total synchronicity with other birds without speaking in words. Nature does not, nor will ever follow human logical reasoning!

We are connected to all things and perfection is found in each of us. So the question is, do you know what you are capable of naturally doing without your head getting in the way? How would you discover this about yourself?

If you observe everything around you, you will learn everything you need to know about self-trust and courage. Our environment is a demonstration of what we are able to do and create yet we believe the only way we can do it, is go to our brain and start thinking it. When you need to go to the toilet you do not think about it, you just go to the toilet! Trust your inner guide, just like you respond to your need to urinate or change your body position. You just know. Trust it, listen, and then do it! Then the more you trust the more your courage will flourish.

If your arm is getting stiff and you know you need to move it, you just do it automatically. You don't think about it, right? There are many things you naturally do, that you do not need to think about, because you trust your system to take care of you and, because it is intelligent, it works with you. You have an intelligent body and it is wired up to your natural energy, which is also known as your spirit or the real you! Who is the "you" that your body belongs to?

Are you only your nose, your arms, your legs, and your body parts? Is that just who you feel you are? Even if you are not particularly spiritual, you know that you are more than your physical body. Do you feel a certain consciousness, sometimes a certain connection with the living, and what is around you, what is often called spiritual awareness?

There is no such thing as security, no such thing as guarantees. Everything is always changing and nothing is ever secure. We

just try and convince ourselves that it should or could be despite constant reminders that everything keeps changing and rarely stops for long. We still like to hold onto that illusion, why is that? It does not have to be that way most of the time.

Breathing is so important. You must do everything that makes you breathe more because that is your key to self-connecting and getting rid of those illusions. It simply kicks us into awareness. Breath finds you wherever you are. It is the gift that makes us special. It does not matter where you are, it finds you. You do not find it! You do not pay for it, not yet, thank God. It finds you and you take it in and you enjoy it. Take in more breath and you will feel better, you'll feel healthier, you'll feel stronger, you'll feel more alert, you'll feel more courageous and you'll feel much more present to do things that will surprise you. When we are sleeping our bodies take over. We breathe properly and deeply compared to when we are awake, and all those triggers and bad conditioning restrict our breathing and mean we use less than 20% of our lung capacity. What would happen if we used that other 80% of our breathing potential? It is an odd metaphor – but maybe there is a correlation to the percentage of the real us that is usually missing. When we are shadow of ourselves and we have gone into our heads maybe we are only 20% of who we truly could be?!

Do we really expect to conquer or fight most diseases or things that make us feel unwell if we are only running at 20%? How is that going to be possible if we are under resourced (low immune system)? If we are running on a shallow lung capacity but expect our body to give us maximum energy, wellness, and clear thinking, how will this happen exactly? Remember that motion and exercise improve breathing...

We automatically breathe more deeply when we exercise. We create higher energy, detoxify, and cleanse the body while moving and breathing. When you move and breathe, you go into higher frequency energy and it is very hard in that state to feel down, to feel powerless, or to not be in the present moment. When you engage motion and breathe consciously you will have more awareness, more power, more sense of presence, more relevant 'now' points of reference with your instincts, your thoughts and your organs. When we are thinking we restrict our motion, we restrict our breath.

Remember and observe, then do!! When we are restricting these two things we are messing with ourselves. We feel terrible, especially if you maintain this for long periods of time like so many of us do! In doing so, you inevitably fall sick (maybe very sick), you will start feeling unwell, have a low frequency energy, become irritable and won't be happy. Why? Because you are restricting your motion and your breath with probably very little live water and you are probably not even consciously aware of it!

Unbreakable Through Motion, Water and Breath

Motion, water, and breath are essential to our being. These basic practical things are usually overlooked and not taken seriously but without them we would not be here. I have repeated this again and again because we are so often stubborn! We know these basic things are crucial and what do we do? We do the opposite! What makes that so? I do not know! Maybe we like pain?!

The over complicated secret…

Just breathe, drink live water, eat live food, move, and be silent at least once a day, in thoughts and words! That is the biggest secret that has been so over complicated. I've now shown you the simple ways to get to your natural peak state, wellness, awareness, power and higher frequency energy to do more and be happy just for the hell of it…. so anything extra becomes a wonderful present. If you cannot manage to do these five necessary things, the most important is to breathe consciously. That is the number one! It is even more effective when you are in water, having a bath, taking a shower or swimming in the sea or lake…

A visual example to help: In your mind's eye see yourself sitting down in the shower, warm water is running down on you, you breathe deeply from your stomach feeling the calming warmth, the strokes of the shower like rain… with real, deep breathing coming from your stomach, and the middle part of your chest, by the end of your shower, you will feel calm and refreshed.

When you consciously breathe, you will become aware and, in so doing, eliminate most of your problems, as your truth will rise and your illusions will be seen for what they are more clearly. You will have more natural wellness than you can ever imagine. You do not have to go into deep meditation or yoga. Everyday, we have rituals such as walking our dogs, running up steps, our daily chores…find in these moments time to actively consciously breathe…. and drink live water.

People will want to be around you, because your energy frequency is high, inviting, and attractive. Try it; you really have nothing to lose. When we do these basic things, we are more than half way to better decisions, better wellness, feeling good and just having a sense of being present, a sense of being aware.

Observe your old habits that do not help you…

Pay attention or observe your habits. I call them habits, because they are not something we do naturally or were born with but they are unhelpful habits we form and have made up over the years. They rarely get updated or checked to see if we should still buy into them…

CHAPTER 9

LOOKING AT YOUR LIFE. CAN YOU CALL IT A BLESSING?

Listening to your heart moves you in the right direction without having to think is this right or wrong! Consciously listen and follow your heart and, with your backbone, go where it takes you. Courage is guaranteed when you live in the uncertainty of life as mindless fear will eventually leave you and genuine fearlessness will take over. It is an amazing feeling.

Does it feel right to blindly follow rules imposed on you from the outside? Aren't rules made by people who want to rule you? I see most rules as a guide, some you must follow but they are not the things that make us real! To blindly follow rules is certainly not the truth. History has taught us enough about following rules.

You will know it when you listen. Even Jesus, Buddha, Krishna or Mohammed did not always follow rules! They did their heart's will. We must be our own light, even a little candlelight at the start; it will always show or light the way for you. This is better than complete darkness and feeling lost most of our lives, because we are living someone else's life. It is easy to look outside of ourselves but it is about time we opened up our own closed door and go inside our home, using the keys we have always had, but perhaps lost along the way. Perhaps we were not ready for whatever reason. Your answers have always been at home waiting rather than outside where you have been looking for them!

Never be a copy or an imitator, be original and follow your own script tailored to your heart's dialogue and not what you have been programmed to do. Break through your mind's dialogue based on old past data that is mostly fear based and unhelpful. You can do this through genuinely listening to your heart's dialogue. Just start anywhere with the basic keys I have outlined… forget about right or wrong or the best way to begin that is just another delay of your mind.

Leading with your heart life will keep you close to your source, spirit, and true self, but definitely away from your thinking mind. Your thinking mind is not who you are. Search within yourself in your own home, so you can be clear on what you feel is true for you. Sometimes, to get to your true home, you may knock on the wrong doors. That is ok. The journey to your life is, and will always be, in the process. The end result is just a plus and besides it usually turns out differently to how we thought it would be anyway!! It is funny how your God or the universe sometimes has other plans for you. To create your genuine true life you will learn, from experience, that you just have to relax. You will realise you have done it before. It is nothing new and you will feel alive, even in the unknown, by following your own heartfelt guide!!

The beauty is when you enter your own home, you will just know. Thinking is never needed. All efforts contribute to your ultimate passion, on what feels true to you, and your true growth. This is your journey to your everyday joy and happiness in the moment. Your purpose is in the moment. Like your purpose now is reading this book. Life is always changing. It is never stagnant. By the time a rule or commandment is issued, those rules or commandments are already outdated. Our life flows like water. You just need to flow with it. What does that mean? Begin with the breath!

"Go wherever your heart takes you first, not your head."
Zen Tao's Teaching.

Break free, let go like a butterfly in the wind. A butterfly that is so light but still never gets blown away. How is that possible? Do you feel or think the butterfly follows a rule? Alternatively, is it following its natural intuitive guide, some sort of uncensored inner guide? Yes, uncensored. How else can some butterflies fly for thousands of miles with a brain smaller than a few grains of sand.

Life is unknown, one cannot always prepare for it, no matter how much you would like to have the upper hand. This is why it is a must to build up your backbone rather than your "wishbone". Your "wishbone" will never prepare you for life. It just shrinks you. Soon enough you will realise you cannot control it. Sadly, it is usually when too much time has passed and we are full of regrets, fear or bitterness.

Gratitude, Clarity, and Then Wisdom!

We have a lot of doubt, which means we try and fit in, join the queue lines led by rules, made years ago. We never learn or draw from our own guide and trust ourselves as a start. If we do not even trust ourselves, what else have we got and why should anyone else trust us?

We have no choice but to come back home to ourselves to deal with what is happening. Most people only put their house in order and live their truth towards the last days or months of their lives. Why on earth must we wait till our body packs up to address this? It happens because we get too comfortable, purposeless and bored in our heads most of the time. I know it sounds depressing, but it needs to be said for you to really be your own guide...

How else do people from Africa, and other developing countries, have a better inner quality of life and attitude than us in the Western World. Yet they have very few comforts compared to us, their life is much tougher but they relate to it differently by accepting it with gratitude and making it better somehow! I know this as I have lived in Africa for many years and extensively travelled in other developing countries. A simple example, whenever I visit countries like Nigeria, Kenya or Gambia, there would often be a power cut while we are eating or watching TV … the local people just bring out the candles, start laughing and joking about the power company etc. and generally make a nice social fun occasion out of the power cut. They do not freak out or feel like their whole world has just stopped unlike many in the West who would immediately start complaining. They would never think about using it as an opportunity to perhaps connect or socialise with their neighbours!

Crucial Recap

If it is at all possible, pack your bags once a year and take a holiday in those types of countries. Meet the people and live their lives for a short while. I promise you, when you get back home you will really appreciate and be more grateful for the things you have. It will almost feel like you have won the lottery…

"People are always blaming circumstances for what they are. I do believe in circumstances. The people who get on in this world are the people who get up and look for the circumstances they want, and if they cannot find them, make them."
George Bernard Shaw

CHAPTER 10

OPEN INTELLIGENCE, THE ULTIMATE WISDOM TO ALL TRUTHS… THAT OPENS OUR THINKING HEART…

Intelligence is aliveness, it is spontaneity. It is openness, it is showing vulnerability, and it is impartiality. It is the courage to function without conclusions.

What is our version of intelligence?

We generally think logically and that what we read in books or study at university makes us intelligent. However, your ability to repeat or rely on what I call your head's library is not what really matters. What matters is what you do with it next that is true and genuine.

We can access so much information so easily nowadays so why is it that pure courage is needed to use your intelligence in an open none conclusive way? Simply, because when you come to a "conclusion" you believe this conclusion protects you. You have a false sense of security. How does this happen? And how can we live in the clouds everyday, only to be hugely disappointed? Our sense of safety and security gets shattered and yet we keep at it blindly.

The alternative is listening to your own intelligent heart that knows what keeps you alive, makes you feel and live genuinely, while growing. Your heart is not just for pumping blood! Scientific evidence shows the contrary as mentioned before. People with heart transplants have memory flashes and develop tastes of their heart donor. Think about why it is that when you fall in love or are doing something that truly deeply feels so good you feel it in your stomach or heart? What else might it be? Search for your own truth within yourself and you decide. But, ask the question, what do I feel is my truth from my heart? Then wait for your reply. You may not always like what you hear. However, your genuine inner response means that you have engaged all your senses, including only the thoughts that you need in that moment.

Unfortunately, pure thinking, without engaging all your senses, turns out to be usually fear based if the mind or head dialogue has anything to do with it. It is never helpful except if you consciously decide to think towards what you are truly for...

Therefore, it is easier to ask questions of your heart and get a reply. This is very different from what we could have ever thought possible. Ask the questions anyway and you will get a reply... feel what happens next.

'No mind' opens all doors, new ways and creativity!

We somehow think that excessive thinking will give us what we want but in reality, 'No Mind' opens possibilities. How do you feel? Has excessive thinking created blessings in your life and brought you peace and genuine contentment?

We were born with one mind before (through continuous doubtful thoughts and pre-conditions from society, family and friends) it was plugged into so many minds… via excessive thinking and many distractions on important but not immediate things to deal with, although we plug into it all to try and sort it all at once (creating more anxiety).

This behaviour makes us forget and lose our natural ability to sense and be guided to do what is genuine and true naturally. Birds do not think to fly. They just fly. Trees do not think to grow, they just do it. The same goes for virtually every other living thing including the earth itself. It spins and flies at the same time. Imagine if our heart or kidneys doubted themselves and decided to think for a while before doing what they are naturally meant to do. We would be in serious trouble!

So it stands that if we were born with a 'No Mind', then our excessive unhelpful mind thinking is just a product of our social conditioning (TV; school; university; radio; religion, government, friends, groups, family etc…). You should be guided from your own heart, which you feel speaks to you clearly. Remember how you felt when you were truly free at heart like a child. Our journey back to ourselves can then begin again. The funny thing is we call this change but actually, it is the opposite, we are coming back to our true natural state. This state has always been there. We just never tapped into it or accessed ourselves as we were living far away in our head dialogue and drama for so long, pretending to live our lives.

What has been your true feeling when someone tells you they are trying to do something? Do you have any belief or confidence in them trying? In my experience trying is a spineless word that evokes no action at all. It is like a kind of way out, a way to not doing something. It is the kind of 'BS' we tell ourselves. It really means we are not really bothered or that we are scared we could let others or ourselves down!

Thinking cannot know the unknown or have an idea of how it truly relates to you. Only your heart's dialogue can come close. Your heart knows you and your body so much better than your conditioned head (which can only put together old data and project it into the future). You have to consciously say what will help you or will make you feel good and choose to think about it. Call it "conscious thinking". Truth is derived from an experience or inner guide. Thinking usually comes from a belief (heard, told, put there unknowingly or knowingly). Remember that everything is a guide; you decide "heart fully" first, then go from there.

The truth cannot be learnt from studying. You can read about great sex or an amazing place. But the truth will only show itself to you when you actually experience it from inside yourself, in your own home, so to speak. The map of a place is never the place itself. The place shows itself to you when you are there and you experience it for yourself.

Let's be honest now, how many times have you seen a movie or read something or listened to the news, judged and made up your mind about it, him, her, a group, a place using lots of past data assumptions? Before you came to a conclusion based on someone else's experience, had you ever come anywhere close or experienced it? Yet, we all have different experiences in the same situation. In fact it is a rare thing for two individuals to experience something in exactly the same way, even something as dramatic as a car accident - there may have been two people there at the same time but both will have different pictures, movies and sounds of what happened.

In the same way you will never find two exact individuals. We are all born and we will all die and yet we are all unique. It is a strong message from your God - or the universe or whatever you believe in - that we are here to create and experience for ourselves and contribute from our own unique gifts no matter how small.

I have always maintained that God or whatever created us, regardless of your beliefs, has an amazing sense of humour. Look at how wonderfully varied we all are as human beings. There is only one of you, even when you look similar to someone else. Is that not incredible?! Yet, we like to continually compare ourselves to others or groups. Why on earth is that exactly? How does that help us? And where exactly are the growth, learning and experience in that? What purpose does it serve you? Ask your heart or gut and wait for your reply - I lovingly dare you!

Isn't it funny that the more you think, the more you lose your sharpness or grasp on whatever you are thinking about. What makes this so? The mind delays most things, slows us down when we spend too much time there, not to mention the health or body degeneration it causes (unhelpful destructive thoughts). Your true self or your inner dialogue is your best guide or friend (trust your heart and your gut that has not learnt doubt yet unlike your brain or mind!).

You will get a better response and not a fear based reaction. You will get love from your inside towards what must be done or decided. In fact, the opposite of love is fear. It was never hate. When one is not fearful, one connects with most things. Think back to the time when you did not judge people or groups. It is a tough one, right?! Let me help. Remember a recent disaster e.g. the London terrorist bombing in 2005, or the 2005 Tsunami in Thailand or even the recent devastating flooding in Pakistan 2010. We did not know these people, we had not read about them as individuals, yet we felt their pain and sympathised with sincere love for them. Where did this come from exactly?

I give this example again - you are walking down the street, thinking or worrying to yourself, when you see a child fall over, or worse still you witness an accident in which someone is hurt. You automatically forget what you were thinking about and your automatic response is to help without thinking, no matter what race or colour they are. This is our known heart, the large part of us that is connected to others, even to strangers. So why do we keep thinking we are so separate from everyone else?

Is this a case, in our true experience, of love and connection? This experience relates to you and every human being (not human thinking!), from any nation, race or culture in the world. No words are necessary, no label or tag needed for unconditional love, connection and empathy to help others.

Excessive thinking leads to filling up with junk food with no nourishing nutrients - a bit like going to McDonalds. Think about your car. It uses petrol as a nutrient to drive for longer and better. I dare you to put the wrong type petrol in it at the filling station and see what happens! Yet, we do it with ourselves!

For me, when my heart is free, my mind is usually light. The intensity, focus and joy of being in that moment with that experience must never be lost or forgotten! But it will be lost through excessive thinking. We let the stranger within us take us over even if it is not intentional but conditioned. Has thinking been fulfilling for you? Has it deeply helped you to feel good and grow? Has it really helped you show love? Pause, stop and ask your heart or gut or whatever body part speaks to you the loudest (apart from your head!). How do you ask your heart? By saying, "Do I feel this is true deep down in my heart or gut?" or "Do I genuinely feel it is true that…?".

You will benefit more from shifting power through asking helpful questions. They give clarity towards manifesting or creating. They allow effortless living while connecting and experiencing genuine love for others and ourselves. We finally get to be our own best friend first! God knows, most of us do not treat ourselves as well as we treat our best friends or those we truly love. Why not?

There is great power in asking helpful questions and in creating our own short powerful way to actually do our heart's will. It stops us from delaying acting and doing what we deeply must do. The questions shifts us beyond our normal conditioned beliefs towards our heartfelt dreams or desire. We will no longer use someone else's life script and quotes, or working for someone else's dreams.

I have not only applied this in my life, but have seen how so many of my clients have been astounded by the impact it has had on their major problems, many of which they have been trying to solve for years.

Logical Thinking Rule Our Lives! Is This True For You?

Let us look at some scientific facts relating to how we become conditioned. Let us look at the how our minds are constantly filled up with stuff, loads of unhelpful trash. Trash that needs dumping, a bit like junk mail or computer viruses. We need to delete them, we need to use our virus checker, otherwise the whole computer will simply crash. We all know how much of a delay and cost that brings to us.

If you look around you, at your TV, the elevator, planes, your toothpaste, the electric toothbrush, the fast cars, etc. Scientists will probably have concluded at some point that it was impossible to go further with these inventions, yet someone else has searched within themselves, out of mind and then created something that takes science to the next level.

This step up was not usually from thinking. It was from creativity. And creativity comes from listening to our inner guide; a kind of calling that will not go away. It is your heart thinking out loud – some people call it instinct. These ideas come from nowhere, from nothingness! Is that not amazing? Yet, we continue to think it comes from our thinking alone, even though thinking is much harder work.

Another mystery, that is far from logical, 6-7 weeks after conception a baby's heart 'appears' out of nowhere. Ask any top scientist or doctor today – it remains a complete mystery as to how the heart appears. This is incredible, isn't it, and very illogical? Yet, we continue to behave as though our answers are the result of our thinking. In other words, we believe we cannot get any answers without thinking. How ignorant and silly does that seem now, knowing what we already see and experience around us. I am sure most of us do not like to lie to ourselves that would be out of the question for most of us, right?

I wonder whose idea it was, that we must always think about everything until we figure it out? Whose framing or thinking are we trying to shape things into or fit into? Usually it is someone else's, rather than our own. Yet we think it is all so logical and scientific. This is what science can only conclude. How many times has our best guess so far been proven to not be the case at all? Look around at the evolution of thinking that came from inspired individuals, spirited enough to give us the gift of their heart-full truth and passion they could no longer suppress. What has happened to your own genuine truth or passion that comes from all your senses, your inner created intelligence? It is far less work, not so damn noisy and much quicker once you get into the flow of it.

Learning to access your genuine self and inner secrets I guarantee will surprise you once you've learnt not to be afraid of what may come from it and play there more often – play with that unknown, non-thinking huge part of you!

And yet, we like to conclude and stick to facts that make thinking correct even though we do not actually trust it deep down! Hence, we doubt things most of the time, especially ourselves. We simply need to start by asking, "What do I feel about it?" not "What do I think about it?" and you will start getting genuine answers, the ones that will feel more true to you! This will, without a doubt, create deep roots for your own self-trust. When you trust your inner guide, you will build your power and your natural confidence. You are not your mind, nor are you just the answer to your unhelpful or stressful thoughts. Say no to the mind spinning and worries! Ask questions, it is a good start in diffusing the limiting load we carry in our minds! There is "no thing" like stress, it does not exist, only stressful thoughts we allow again and again, playing in our minds like broken records! Time to nudge it forward and play the rest of our tune. Would you not say?

Breathe life with your heart and stay light in mind!

The "Aaah-Meditation"

When we hear the word meditation, most people automatically picture someone sitting, crossed legged and thinking. They picture allowing yourself a certain amount of time to go somewhere with your mind as you sit quietly doing nothing, just breathing until you find your clarity and inner calm. Well, yes, this can definitely be powerful and healing, but unless you are already able to sit quietly by yourself for long periods of time, this will be a self-defeating way to start meditating.

So, if you are not there yet, fear not. Let us start with some other simple ideas. The "aaaah"-sound is a meditation mantra that is over 2000 years old. It is used for manifesting and creating but it is also extremely useful for quietening one's mind and body, plus you feel the vibration of the sound through your body. This meditation allows you to come back to one's self.

Another meditation mantra for grounding and healing is Ohm. Repeating the sound of 'ohmmm' and feeling its vibration frequency in the body will help you find your calm centre where healing begins. One can achieve the feeling qualities of the 'ohmmm' frequency by watching the sky at dusk, or observing the changing phases of the moon. We are connected to ohm, as ohm is connected to the earth.

Repeat these mantras loudly, so you can feel the frequency of the sound and the effects on your body. Say it like you mean it, so your body and system receives it. The vibration for both meditations will quieten your thinking mind, sending vibrations up and down your chakras, from your spinal chord to your head, through the body energy power line! It is very calming and healing…

As I've mentioned before, meditation can be done in so many situations such as when you are walking up the stairs, washing your plate in the sink, feeling the warm water from the shower run down your body, like warm rain, cleansing and washing away all your troubles.

These simple things, you take for granted, can be used for meditation. All you need to do is just be aware in that moment and feel it without thinking. Or just focus on whatever works for you to move you away from your head thoughts (although focus on your deep breathing brings you back and works better). Let that moment be your only purpose! You will feel at home again, doubtless, calmly powerful and fully present while being aware of your calm deep breathing. This is worth doing more than reading a book or taking a course.

Why? This is simply because most of your problems in your head will not be able to seed themselves if you are mostly in the 'now state'. This can be achieved by making each moment your purpose, while consciously aware of your breathing. What I always say is just do it…you have nothing to lose!

Meditation leads one to listen to your effortless truthful dialogue from your heart and more. Meditation allows the observer and the observed to become one. It takes you to the mystery of the unknown, the source, the space, the field of undefined possibilities, where you connect as pure energy with everything around you.

Most of us have all experienced an overwhelming feeling of love for another, or fierce passion for music or sports, that may even make you shed a tear or two and then you feel a sense of release. This makes us come alive again as it invokes our soul searching and we let go of all our suppressed head thinking unhelpful stuff!

"Science is the murder of mystery. If you want to experience the mysterious, you will have to enter through another door, from a totally different dimension."
OSHO

Meditation opens one of these doors.

Open a new door to your being. Be who you are, but also, be aware of how multi-faceted you are. We hold so many mysteries. If, for example, you are a scientist, while in the lab be a scientist. When out of the lab, be aware and be open to the unknown mysteries of who you are. We are all one! We are limitless. Take claim of who you are and the unknowing part. We actually do know many things, we have just forgot. Tap into your greatness! Look at all our inventions and creations deemed to be impossible before, until someone listened to their own truth and power.

We all have this natural super-self. It is a matter of being aware of it and embracing our power and our inner source. That is all there is to it! It needs no complications. Why play down whom you really are? I have noticed that even the reality TV shows, such as the "X Factor", encourage people to be more than their shadow self even if initially it's just for fame and fortune. However, it is a start. It is never just about motivation. It is always about how big and important our reasons are - they kick us into action much more!

What is your purpose now?

It is amazing being in the moment. Our purpose is whatever we are doing right now or observing then and there. This is what being in the present is all about. Its mystery unravels itself to you and the observer becomes the observant. Become a child again in your heart to experience your moments. That is why children have such a great time doing almost anything. Our experience will never be the same again, even if you try to go back and recreate it exactly. It will always be different. That constant change is the amazing mystery of life ... something that science can never fully explain!

How do you know exactly what your purpose is now, without all the fuss?

First Step:

Become like the water; flexible, flowing, moving, effortlessly patient, penetrating and irresistible.

Be quiet and be still.

Observe a sunset.

Observe children playing.

Sing out loud.

It is in these moments, when you are connected to yourself that you should ask the questions. Be patient; allow your spirit to respond. You will find the answers you have been searching for.

Let me ask a few self-trust questions. As ever, be honest and make sure you write your answers down.

1. What makes me not trust myself on most things?
2. What makes me feel people do not trust me, if brutally honest?
3. What must genuinely happen for me to doubt less and trust more?

List all your answers. The answers will help you gain clarity towards what you now choose.

Doubt comes from the insecurity in us, spun by our so-called head intelligence, not our heart's intelligence. It is usually fear based.

What makes us lack the confidence to trust or even be trusted? Is it because we doubt ourselves and think we will disappoint or let others down, including ourselves?

We can only bullshit ourselves for so long. Eventually we must face our truth; otherwise it will knock our doors wide open to let everything else we do not want in.

Ask yourself has your unhelpful stressful thinking or fear-based

Be Surprised

thoughts really brought you to a place of joy and happiness in your heart. If the honest answer is yes, then please do carry on!

If your answer it no, then please listen up and let's switch you on to your own expert guide, your heart's dialogue, your pure effortless intelligence. It is for your benefit!

When you can access your genuine heart's intelligence, you get to live in the unknown with far less fear! Best to start by doing what you love to do. We think far less, and of nothing else, when we are absorbed in doing something we love. It really gets us focused, enthused usually with drive. What do you feel makes this so?

Think back to the past when you were in love with whatever experience you were having. It filled your heart with genuine joy. Where were your unhelpful thoughts then, the so-called doubtful thinking thoughts at that time? They were nowhere to be heard. Trust that lightness, how alive you felt and observe how your mind had no charge on you. In these moments, your mind, body and spirit work together effortlessly towards whatever you are creating enthusiastically from your heart!

You are the one experiencing your choices and journeys. So best to get to know your heart felt truth, for your own benefit. Do not be half there, do not sleep walk through life. Embrace life and own your truth! How great would that feel to own your truth?

Your heart knows you, it beats to your rhythm (fear, joy, excitement, laughter etc.) every second! It always changes its rhythm to match whatever you are experiencing, it knows you without doubt, it is not conditioned like our minds, nor has it learnt doubt. Please, get this simple thing, right here, right now… for you, no one else!!!

Trust it and never stay with your doubtful thoughts. Your heart's intelligence will respond to your challenges as they occur and you will handle them all. Your light will come out.

The sooner we listen with our hearts, the quicker our pain, doubt and regrets will pass. It is crucial if you want clarity, joy and growth, to ask the questions needed but also answer without blame, analysis or judgement. Do not hold onto your past history or drama, do not keep repeating the same unhelpful pictures, movies and sounds of the situation. We usually feel distressed when our mind is charged unhelpfully and led by our stranger. This will not free you up, it will only lock you down. Remember that this is truly where the juice of life exists. Ask anyone who lives life genuinely!

So, let it out, speak your heart's dialogue and respond. Stop over reacting, so you do not get lost yet again. It is always up to you. So, choose to listen to your heart's dialogue naturally. Sometimes, we just need a bigger reason to want to listen to ourselves. We get so comfortable and complacent that we do not feel it necessary to take action. Hence, usually some crisis has to happen to push most of us to take action.

Nothing came and comes naturally except perhaps breathing, sleeping and going to the toilet. We had to learn everything. We had to learn how to walk, talk, move, sit, dress ourselves, wash ourselves, tie our shoes, ride a bicycle, brush our teeth, even how to eat with spoons and knives. The basic list is endless. Yet, we forget so quickly and think we cannot possibly do or learn anything else we may love to do! So guess what, we rarely learn our basic natural self-trust skills on top of what we know already. They are rarely repeated often enough - unlike everything else we do – to enable them to become part of our daily good habits… like learning to breathe properly, listening to what our body is truly telling us etc.

"Follow your heart, your dreams, your desires. Do what your soul calls you to do, whatever it is, and allow it to be finished; then you will go on to another adventure.

You will never be judged unless you accept the judgement of those around you.

And if you accept their judgement, it is only your will to do so for the experience"
Ramtha

"There are many living far below their possibilities because they are continually handing over their individualities to others."

Do you want to be a power in the world? Then be yourself.

Be true to the highest within your soul and then allow yourself to be governed by no customs or conventionalities or arbitrary man-made rules that are not founded on principle."
Ralph Waldo Trine

CHAPTER 11

THE BEST GIFT…

As it has been said, the best gift you can bring to this world is the gift of you. You are unique in the world, no one else is like you, no one else has your exact gifts. What is also unique is when you are living your magic you feel like you are glowing from the inside out. When you are genuine and have shed off your masks you are connected to your source, your light. What is possible at this point? What is your energy like? Is it possible to continuously create new possibilities?

It will surprise you! Listen to your heart's dialogue, and then just do it and see. I promise you, you will be alive when you do it. You will be in knowing, not thinking, as it just feels damn right and you do not know why sometimes. There are no accidents or coincidences in life. Life is perfection, whether, we want to see it or not…it just is.

"Many false steps were made by standing still"
Fortune Cookie

"Named must your fear be, before banish it you can…"
YODA, from Star Wars, The Empire Strikes Back

Hero Within or the Shadow in the Background?!

If you can manage the key actions outlined so far in this book, you will have an enormous amount of wellbeing and you will come back to yourself frequently. In addition, when you come back to yourself you will do a lot more. You will be resourceful, with more inner strength, you will be running on a higher frequency. Even your social life will improve, as people generally like being around individuals or groups with such inviting energy. Things will naturally come to you more effortlessly. You will know and can do more, much more. It is your own natural power. I call this natural power the hero in you, the superman or superwoman in you. I used to love comic books when I was a kid, particularly "Spiderman", and "The Silver Surfer". I enjoyed reading these comics because I truly believed on some level that we also had such super powers.

Superman was another super hero that fascinated me because he created an outer image of himself to fit in. Clark Kent is actually superman's costume! He created an outer shell or costume, which revealed all his other sides - weakness, vulnerability, non-courageous, doubtful sides. Superman was born superman, he was never somebody else, but when he put on his costume, he became the weaker part of himself. He made the costume to fit in and be accepted, so others would not feel threatened. Guess who pops out when there is a major crisis that needs a more determined approach? Who do you really become when your crisis or challenges shake things up? Is your costume on or off?

Society does not seem to take kindly to creative, high-energy individuals or great doers. Many people feel threatened by the great "movers and shakers" of this world. They lack the awareness of their own personal power and are threatened by others who may exercise theirs. Many historical great leaders have been killed or betrayed only to become saints, or praised after their death. They are remembered by what they have achieved perhaps at a high price. We all know that society can be fickle, so we restrain ourselves. Remember that society is likely to dislike us or fear us, no matter what we do or do not do. So, do not give up on one's truth in order to be accepted, it is truly a waste of one's time and energy. We should be spending more time in our own natural state, as our own natural resourceful hero. How else are we going to get to know ourselves in that brilliant, feel-good resourceful state?

When you breathe, when you move, when you engage your body with a healing massage, when you go meditate, go for walks, all these experiences will bring you back to your super self. Your natural bold self exists; you just do not stay there naturally without a push, as it is not a common place for most of us.

The place to be is your hero self. You will draw amazing creativity including connectivity with people. You will tap into your inner strength, invincibility and greatness. You know those times when you fully engage with yourself and deliver amazing ideas that **surprise even you**. I am talking about those experiences that extend you beyond your thought possibilities. Most of us have been there, where it has been a natural high, where you just felt **good, despite** your initial fears. Doing the things that get you back to your resourceful state is key. Remember those experiences such as when you were talking with your friends, feeling good, enjoying those magic moments, hugging somebody, making love to somebody, going for a walk somewhere beautiful, by a river, climbing a mountain with amazing views that takes your breath away, looking at the snow when you're skiing, diving or swimming, enjoying a spa, reading something great or inspiring, feeling the sensation of a great massage, listening to your most inspiring music and so on….

All those things… remember them… and certainly do them more for your own benefit. Other people will certainly benefit by default one way or another. Repetition helps to ground you. So, stay engaged with yourself and your own genuine inner guide, as you are truly your own expert. Do not stay with your unhelpful thoughts that switch you off and kick those desires out of your life! When they come, recognize them, but choose another thought. One that will raise your energy. We have this opportunity at any given time.

Here is a little secret from one of my favourite writers who wrote this inspiring verse. It has become part of my life's script. I also use it to remind myself to get back to my basics and always start from there no matter what. I wonder what YOUR true verse will be in your own life's script?!

"I went to the woods because I wanted to live deliberately… I wanted to live deep and suck out all the marrow of life! To put to rout all that was not life… and not, when I come to die, discover that I had never lived!!"
Henry David Thoreau

The above quotation inspired me to write the following:

Building one's backbone and not a wishbone is the source and beginning of a life well travelled.

Here is the thing, it is very important to get to see all the beauty and immediate things we have in our lives. The sure way to do this is to travel somewhere, somewhere where things are very basic, like Africa or Asia. Try and go camping for at least 2 weeks every 6 months. I promise you, it will be like all your things are brand new when you get back! If at all possible, it is better to go for longer (6 weeks), as it takes the mind awhile to unravel from all that adverse unhelpful conditioning. Then you will really get to know what coming back to your self, loving and valuing the things you take for granted, means. Yes, courage and self-trust could lead you to take some risks but they are needed to make you grow and blossom.

You will fall and rise many times. It is best to choose where your heart leads you. If you love doing whatever you choose your approach will be different for sure. Let us face it, things only really become a problem when we are not that interested. Think or decide where you are now, and where you want to go in this lifetime. Regrets are a terrible thing to have to live with. Choose your life or someone else will choose it for you.

CHAPTER 12

BUILDING A BACKBONE, NOT A WISHBONE!

As well as developing a backbone, using our intelligent heart and relying less on our doubtful head, what are the other alternatives that lead us back to our genuine self quicker and keep us more rooted longer term? If you think hard enough you will remember when you experienced things you just cannot explain but you just knew that they felt very right for you. This self-awareness guide is in all of us. We just simply need to relax our minds to access and listen to our inner dialogue and strengthen that muscle in us. It does not matter what we tag it, it only matters what we do with it and what comes next.

The main thing is that without the response and action it is just memory. What happens when you are alone by yourself and you are sitting on the toilet like anyone else, who are you then? Are you what you do? Are you a doctor, a surgeon, a pilot or the identity we call ourselves? Who are you? Are we truly our jobs? Is this why we are here on the planet? Who is this being? What is my significance?

What would it feel like to be light at heart, unafraid of one's power, eyes wide open and heart full of love and gratitude? One's heart needs to be fully open so you can listen to what it is saying, so you can be aware of the secret inner choices and so our natural intelligence can evolve with all our senses fully alight.

Getting Courage to Shine With Your Heart's Secrets

Where exactly are you now in your life? Where has the real you gone to? What dialogue do you keep playing over and over in your head most of the time? Are you usually in your head or listening to your heart? Be honest with yourself, how else can you trust yourself? Build your own courage and listen to your own heart's secrets. Do simple things first, things that make you feel innocent again, untainted by pride and self-importance, and so you can be open to the good with a pure heart. You must get back to your heart's innocence, be like a child again. You were like this before so you will remember once again. How do you get clarity and trust yourself with all that bullshit noise in your head?

"There is no need to have courage if you are innocent, there is no need either, for any clarity because nothing can be more clear, crystal clear, than innocence"
OSHO

You were born with innocence. You only have the future, no past! Yet we listen and act on prewritten doubts and fears - doubts and fears that are not even ours. From our innocent birth we start to believe other people's conditioned ideas and ways. We tend to pick up their luggage and live with it even though those ideas may not be harmonious to our own mind, body and soul. What makes us do that?

Perhaps because it is supposed to make us clever, smart, give us memories, experiences and expectations so we fit in. What is our real truth, if we are honest? Who are we genuinely when we are alone with ourselves? What makes us stay unfulfilled deep down?

It is like we are in the shadows, never coming out, always with our cup half full (if even that), and we all feel it. It is nothing new! We do not realise that all the success in the world is nothing compared to a future where we feel and use our senses and gifts.

The amazing individuals that have propelled the biggest shift in human awareness, gave us their natural gifts and inner secrets - they just could not suppress them any longer! We can all find these gifts when we start listening to our heart's secrets and less to our head's doubtful dialogue.

The Last Time…

Always remember that whatever you are doing, it could be the last time you do it. We still cannot rewind to our past to change "No thing".

I have met and observed a lot of people that have relocated trying to find themselves, moving abroad to a sunnier place or to the sea. Usually this occurs when it is almost check out time! They finally choose to live their life for the final 10-20% of it. What makes us live 80-90% of our lives spending time on things that never satisfy us or genuinely add anything to our lives? What makes us suddenly want to do the last minute things with what is left of our life? How come we only change when our time is almost up? Why is it only then we listen to our hearts? What makes us wait so damn late before we genuinely live? We have worked for so long only to give it all away in the end.

So, decide what you are living for from the beginning. Think about it!! Do you really want to devote your life to the stuff that will just be given away? Isn't better to concentrate on the things that fulfil one's heart, soul or inner cry? What have you given your genuine real gifts and joys up for? At the end of one's life, do we think about all possessions we have collected over the years or do we think about our family and close friends and if we really truly loved? Do you want to end up regretting that you never shared your real gifts? I know this is hard but time waits for no one. It does not care if you are left behind or not. Do not wait till you retire before you live and listen to your heart's secrets.

The best gift you can give to the world is the gift of the genuine heartfelt you without any "ifs" or "maybes"!

I woke up and began living my own life at the age of 26. Soon after, I also stopped working for other people and I began to pursue my own heart's desire. This was the beginning of my 'salvation', my own soul's journey and living in the mystery or uncertainty of life. It is the most liberating feeling of inner freedom you can imagine. The main thing is to listen to and act on your heart's secrets.

Are You Ever Going To Write Your Own Life Script?

The constant need to possess things, without any genuine heartfelt purpose, corrupts us. We spin on an endless cycle. This cycle keeps us busy and keeps us always wanting more; more money, property, and power. We know, deep down, that we will never be satisfied, and that we will always want more. However, true satisfaction does not come from things we get from the outside world, it can only be reached from within. We are our own experts. We need to make a shift in our focus and go within. Start rewriting your life from the inside out.

Most people's possessions are their false identity, their false sense of living. The ego! If you have guts or courage you will not need a false ego substitute which will always drive you towards wanting more. This clouds your genuine truth.

Whatever I am doing, if I do not know what I am doing it for, it soon becomes meaningless, no matter how much I will try and deny this. Listening to myself, listening to my real voice brings me back to myself. It fulfils my nature, makes me complete daily. When I have stayed with my acting or head's dialogue (my ego) and I keep doing everything that is not really true to my heart and actual nature then I do not genuinely know who I really am. How then can I be genuinely happy?

It is without a doubt a must to first know who you are. Only then can you do something or anything that satisfies your nature. This, and only this, will make you naturally content and feel at home with yourself. Now let us be honest with ourselves. Again, we must understand we are all our own experts.

Have you ever realised who you are by analysing and thinking a lot about yourself? Or do you realise who you are from a deeper inner search? Maybe with the help of some external natural influences? Maybe with the help from nature (sea, lakes, trees, etc.) or a holiday, or a soul-searching experience? Which one has been more true to you? Make sure your head's dialogue does not constantly steal the show of your life so you become the audience instead!

Liking Problems, The Surprises We Don't Like…

Letting go of control we never had in the first place…

What happens when you succeed at something? Why does the feeling not last? Why, when it all goes to plan, do you feel unfulfilled and dissatisfied? It is when we are surprised that we generally start living and growing. Sometimes at the start of something new in our lives, we may feel challenged due to fear and doubt. However, once we walk through it, we gather strength, courage and become surprised. We need surprises and yet some of us hate having them. They fire us up, make us come alive again and deep down we welcome the unknown surprise that breaks our boring repetitive ways. The unknown is where life is and all our senses get awakened and stimulated by being in the now.

" I am always doing things I can't do – that's how I get to do them."
Pablo Picasso

The funny thing is when we are born, we all initially have the same quality of consciousness, integrity, courage and boldness. Then, as we go up in the world, we slowly begin to bargain away pieces of ourselves and we pay with our courage, integrity, and self-respect and worse still with our self-trust. The original us disappears slowly, slowly but surely. This bottomless pit of wanting and getting will never satisfy us. What makes us really do these things? It is really just so we can get some more toys, more acceptance, more love, and identity? Is this what we really live for?

There is a story of a rich man who, despite all his wealth, was fed up and not at peace in his mind. He badly wanted peace of mind but, however much he bought, it never came. So he decided to start out on a new journey and he was advised to give more to charity, build hospitals, serve people, and travel to poor countries to save lives. The rich man followed this advice and did many good deeds but still he did not get peace of mind. He was then told about a wise man, who lived in the middle of nowhere, who had helped many others. So, he went to this small village and asked to see the wise man so he could find peace of mind.

On arrival, the village idiot came to him and said: "I hear you are looking for a wise man. I don't give advice and no one listens to me, but if you seek peace of mind, go to the tree over there in the dark and you will find the wise man who will give you what you want". Although a little concerned, the rich man went to meet the wise man in the dark. He thought the wise man looked rather young but nevertheless listened to him as he said: "I can give you peace of mind. What do you carry close to your heart there in your carriage bag?" The rich man said: "Gold, diamonds and more to pay whoever can help me". And the wise man said: "Come down from your high horse and I will give it to you without any doubt". So, he stepped down carefully. As soon as he stepped down, the man grabbed the bag and ran off in the opposite direction. The rich man was shocked and could not believe it at first but he soon realised he had been robbed.

Panicking, he tried to get back on his horse but he fell so he began running after the thief instead. But the old man was too fat and unfit to get close to the young man. He simply could not catch him and the young thief disappeared into the village. The rich man started screaming to anyone he could see "That thief stole most of my valuables, stop him!" He started ranting and talking to himself, saying: "Why did I listen to the village idiot?" The rich man started to cry and was at a loss for words or action.

After sobbing his eyes out, without any help from anyone else in the village, he decided to return to his horse by the tree. When he looked up, there by the tree, was the young man waiting for him by his horse. The rich man was shocked yet again and started screaming at the young man in anger. The young wise man simply said: "Here is your bag". The rich man quickly took it, holding his bag tightly. He was surprised but a bit calmer so he said: "Why the hell did you do that? It was not funny at all!"

The wise young man said: "Well, I wanted to give you back what you already have. But it had to be taken away from you first so you could understand what you already have. This can, and will, eventually happen to you when you least expect it. You got too comfortable and stopped enjoying, seeing, or feeling what you already have! You had forgotten what you already had. You wanted and needed a firm reminder and now you've had it! So, do you have peace of mind now? Stop bothering and disturbing people looking for what you already have got! Are you still worried?"

The rich man felt exhausted but calmly replied: "Thank you". He smiled and got back on his horse. The young man said: "Have you forgotten something? Haven't you forgotten your bag of gold and diamonds?" The rich man smiled again and handed him the bag. He realised he never needed to pay other people for what he already had but he understood it better after paying for it. The old man never forgot what the wise man told him. He went home happier than he had ever been in his entire life as he was now alive and very awake. He looked forward to coming home, to loving and creating happily with what he already had, with a light mind, open heart, gratitude and with no more doubts!

Most of us are in our minds too often and this does not allow for a peaceful heart. If you seek peace then you must seek 'no mind'. You need to get comfortable staying in the unknown to find peace of mind, growth and genuine appreciation. Slow down the mind. Slow it all down and begin to be aware of your surroundings and your thoughts.

We all know what our past looks like, what it feels like. Our future is uncertain, we will never really know what will happen, no matter how much you plan or project. It is worth embracing the unknown. The beauty of life is we have choices. A choice to step into our being. Our unknown is spoken effortlessly from our loyal hearts. We simply need to ask, breathe, wait a little, listen and then do it with passion or enthusiasm again and again. Change the way you look at things, change the way you move, and things will begin to take form. Know that with courage and trust, the unknown will become known and it will be more fun and joyful. One certainly feels more alive and far less afraid or bored! It is an amazing feeling to feel alive.

Do not be concerned by what others think about you. This will only limit you and make you suffer. It will only delay you from stepping up to your true self, your gifts, which are already waiting for you, just waiting for when you are ready! How do you truly feel about that?

"A crank is a man with an idea until it catches on."
Mark Twain

You may be deemed a little crazy but others still like to be around interesting, mad, enthused or spirited people, what makes that so? Other people's differences inspire people. Some get curious and start thinking what else is possible? Sometimes we have to move away from our tribe to move forward so that we can experience our own truth, not our tribe's truth. Take the compliment and be deemed crazy or however they choose to frame you. What it really means is that you will be switched on to experience your true self. Perfection has never been the aim. Understanding who you are and being connected to your being is a daily practice, a way of life.

Perfection is an illusion, completely mind led, making one spend time charged in the head and away from one's self, hurting one's physical body, weakening one's genuine senses and truth. It leads to selling out on one's heartfelt truth. The rewards from loyalty to your heart's truth cannot be put into words!

Most people's self-trust, or ability to listen to their own deeper truth, remains weak. It is easier for them to follow the trend, do what most people do, fit in to what is 'normal'.

How many of us say: "I must have it" or "I need it". The framing of "I need it" justifies and creates the false desire in our thinking mind, which is usually just a short-term fix. In turn it becomes a "need or must have" ego-driven mind charge, a temporary distraction from our other more pressing clearouts. What does it all mean to us really? Are we that bored?

That is why we seek peace of mind, we soul search. Ironically, this occurs more often in the Western World, where we already have much more than we need, and where we are already truly rich, yet we cannot stop feeling like we still lack something.

Most people in the developing world do not have the basic things needed for survival. Yet, they have more peace of mind and a type of wealth that money cannot buy. How do they cope? Could WE cope if we faced the same hell or challenges? Those people are more self aware and appreciative of their lives. This, I believe, comes from them constantly remaining loyal to their hearts often and *'not sweating the small stuff'*. Their self courage their self-trust, meditating or praying to their gods or inner spirit for guidance. They simply must adapt frequently or face a far worse option. Their spirit has truly developed their backbone and not their wishbone! And it is completely free!

CHAPTER 13

FINALLY LETTING GO OF OUR PAST

Finally letting go of our past ...then we have nothing to live up to... then we will truly start to access, see and feel ourselves... like we just met anew!

"Time is an invention. Now is reality. So much creativity is happening for the simple reason that we have withdrawn ourselves from the past and future. Our whole energy remains blocked either in the past or in the future. When you withdraw all your energy from the past and future a tremendous explosion happens. That explosion is creativity."
Bhagwan Shree Rajneesh

Stop living up to the reputation of your past. Think about it. If you let go of your past history, you will have nothing to live up to and nothing to prove. A clean start so you can be aware and listen to your internal guide. One can achieve this by quieting the mind through meditation...

Meditation is simply the courage, yes courage, to be silent and alone. Slowly one starts feeling their genuine self effortlessly come back;

you come alive. Of course, our head's dialogue ego-self will keep trying to distract you, like a child that needs attention, because he or she is bored. Well let it. Eventually it will stay in the background, it will slow down. Meditation quietens the mind. As a first step, get aware of your breathing. Meditation calmly promotes this and you will understand you are the energy observing your body as things occur. It is in the moment we connect with our being that we feel peaceful, resourceful and satisfied. Open your gifts, they are waiting to be expressed and enjoyed.

Although we like things we cannot see and touch, we have all experienced the juice or magic and the beauty of the world coming from the unknown. We have all been astonished or surprised by life at some point...

So how do we feel about death? Do we truly feel that this is the end of us, are we just our body and thoughts alone? Do you honestly feel you are nothing else apart from your body? How does this feel when you check this internally?

Things become clearer one way or another; either through pain, the passing of time, or just being ready to listen to your inner guide. Just stay loyal to your heart's truth, no matter what. It will get clearer. That is the beauty of the real you. You have a choice over what you choose to experience.

You can only lose what needs to be lost. It is like going to the toilet - the more you hold on to it, the more physical discomfort you will receive! Best let it go and experience physical and general well being. Remember that what your body cannot use needs to be flushed away. That is nature's design!

What happens to you when you hold something in for a long period, maybe 1 or 2 days or more? What happens to your eating and sleeping habits? Do you feel better or worse? It is a bit like stopping yourself from going to the toilet and expecting it to just get better or go away. In fact, all you get is more internal discomfort. Even your mind or head dialogue gets out of control and disturbed!

One of my favourite expressions from the movie 'Shawshank Redemption' is: *"Get busy living or get busy dying"*.

I prefer to say: "Get busy living or stay busy dying!"

Whatever reality we choose, it is important to see the quality of how we spend our lives. It does not mean we do not pay our bills and do the normal things. But, how do we spend the majority of our time? It will always be up to you and no one else. Please, make no mistake about that! You came alone and you will leave alone. It is not my intention to burst your bubble. I am just being very clear. I had to get clear with myself at that crucial crossroads in my life. I get it, I truly get it now, and hence I frankly speak my heart's truth! Like the challenging part of life, the bad weather always clears for light to shine through eventually. Enjoy it when you get it, as sometimes it does not stay for long. This again is nature's design. Like a series of tests, and as we pass them in stages to grow, we go high and it can sometimes be even more challenging, and seem totally unfair!

I believe one of the reasons we all must die is for us to remember how unique and precious life is. When someone close to us dies, we do a recheck and value our life more. We get scared and want to embrace life more. What makes us want to hold on to life so much? Even when it is, time to let go? We can only lose what must be lost when our time comes, not just with death or let go of the illusion on control now... The longer it is held tight, the harder it is to let go... Your life can literally get constipated!

To make matters even more challenging, society expects us to behave exactly like one another. This is called being 'normal'. Why is it that learning or remembering to be one's genuine self is called being different? Is this not odd? Should it not be the reverse? The moment one does not act to fit in, people become suspicious of you.

It is unacceptable for you to be your natural self. You must live your life for their version of living not yours.

So, if you condemn yourself, then you are part of normal society, and if you accept yourself deep down, you are out of society or your tribe. However, society still welcomes the amazing gifts and advancement that comes from being your true self, even if they have labelled you crazy! Suddenly you are the hero! Now, is that heart led or mind led? Which will you continue to worship?

Get back to yourself and live your life giving the best gift, the real you, to yourself and to society. Then you and they will love you for it in the end. Deep down everyone loves the greatness of the human spirit and the courage it shines on others to light them up like the stars they truly are.

I have realised that there are many people telling the same mind-led story - it must be true, it is deemed normal! We all like to say how much we want to have a normal life etc, as if it actually existed! Yet this 'normal life' is not something we discuss or look into in great detail if it is true or false. Let us be honest, has this normal life that others live made them truly happy at heart so far? Wanting to be the same as someone else! Most choose to be in the dark their whole lives. Always listen to your own inner compass, as you are truly your own expert, when you are genuinely ready! Keep an open mind and heart. So one listens, experiences, remembers and learns to make one's own blue print.

We seek out people to tell us what to do and so we follow their script, no matter how uncomfortable it might be! Usually it is fear driven. That way you never have to write or design your own script that comes from your inner source or spirit. It means you never have to be responsible for yourself in any deep form, which is where living really exists. If you had the courage, what would you do differently with your life's script? Surely it is better than repeating someone else's script like a parrot?

I truly feel and believe that to be an individual is the greatest courage of all. When you are passionate about what you do, you automatically serve others and everyone wins. One gets to be very grounded and fearless even when the whole world is against you, as it comes from your heart and only love resides there. How would you love to be remembered? Write it down now. It will give clarity on how you truly choose to live. Your own blue print to your life's script, rather than someone else writing it for you. It will also give you courage and clarity on what is truly relevant to you in your life… your true soul's calling. It has always been there; just switch it on more often.

Are you frightened of being alone or bored by your own company? Do you always feel the need to find something to engage your self or mind? Remember that to just simply be and do nothing for at least one hour daily will get you back home to yourself quicker. Now, ask the question, what makes you frightened or bored with your own company?

Listen and do only your heart's secrets and your courage and self-truth will always follow rather than the constant head dialogue and acting out, that usually takes us into our cave.

When you listen and do your hearts will earlier in your life your physical body will age slower. Stop caring what other people think as you respond to your inner dialogue and not your head's dialogue. You will get more courageous the more you practice.

It has and will always be your doing. No one else will be really responsible for you in the end. Let me remind you again that as we came alone so we will leave alone whether we are done with our journey or not! Best to seek that truth out before one is checked out.

CHAPTER 14

HOW TO ACCESS YOURSELF WHEN LOST!

Well it has been said before, but it's always good to remind ourselves again; a key life lesson is to accept self responsibility for all our doings whether they have helped us, others or neither. Then let go of your fearful thoughts, checking them and observing what makes us hold on to them? Do they serve any purpose for us now?

"I had the blues because I had no shoes, until upon the streets, I met a man who had no feet"
Anonymous

Count Your Blessings Constantly – Not Your Troubles!

I use this simple clear sentence to remember my truth and unseen facts everyday! Always stop and deeply ask 'What am I worrying about, if I am really honest? As it is usually unimportant and insignificant on a far smaller scale to your genuine life, we just lose our focus too damn often that is all! It is time to just stop by practising the basics that I have outlined…

- Forgiveness has never been a natural reaction for most of us nor for our ego self. The ego's sense of forgiveness is to look at others as insane or immature. The ego wants the problem to be real and bigger than it is, and then somehow you are the better person. You are the "bigger person" because you can forgive. Even in forgiveness, the ego's secret and silent goal is separation, always to be separated. You are guaranteed this if you, and your ego, are mostly invested in being right! Must that be your only guide? Remember we always feel the discomfort or charge at the start!

- The more you observe yourself without, judgement or blame nor analysis (this is so crucial) the more you will engage yourself and get to know and then trust yourself more. This is true freedom and then genuinely connecting with others comes next without any fuss.

- Change what you must change and do it quickly, no stalling! Accept without blame, bitterness or judgement what you cannot change… or else you will damage or shut down your genuine self all over again.

- Listen to music that gets you back to yourself so you can act or create what you feel deep down. Simply listen to what inspires you or makes you feel good as often as possible.

- Watch movies, comedies etc. that inspire you, or make you laugh, especially when you are the most afraid. This stops the mind spinning a web!

- Read what inspires you as often as possible, so you stay engaged with your higher self, the genuine you. Then operate, create or do from there. You will always be pleasantly surprised!

- Do conscious breathing, frequently. This is the key to it all, no doubt. It secures our grounding firmly in our own home, safe from unwanted guests (unhelpful thoughts, bad health, negative social influencing etc…).

- *"Nothing changes unless something moves"*. Albert Einstein

- Read and observe the individuals that inspire you towards where you choose to go. Spend time with friends and family that celebrate who you are. Waste less time around energies that create limitations, especially if your foundation for self-love is weak. Make your genuine self-love rooted and strong first before exposing yourself to being unintentionally reshaped by others. Walk away and love them from a distance if you must, until you are ready. You are no good to anyone half-baked, or running in your shadow, or worse a complete stranger to yourself, unfulfilled and unhappy.

- List and do all the things you truly love without excessive questioning. Just do and think less, you will always handle the challenges when they do come. Again, remember you have done that many times even if you have forgotten. Lighten the spinning in your head and the resolution will always come to you. Do something to feel good and lighten the load in your head!

- Move your body. Always extend out more frequently rather than deflating or shrinking too often. This makes you unwell and definitely pulls you away from yourself.

- Love and enjoy nourishing live foods more often and treat your self, every now and then, to the tasty but less healthy stuff, never the other way round! Always be responsible for yourself first… always (so your roots hold well). Then you are of real use to yourself or others.

- Blame, judge and analyse as little as possible. Catch yourself when you start before it seeds and plants itself deep. Stop it dead before it grows big fat roots in you! This is slow poison that has no purpose but self-harm.

- Love openly as often as possible, starting with yourself first. Do the things that make you feel love for yourself and others will see love in you and want to be around you and love you naturally, as well. You will shine without even knowing it. It is a beautiful free open feeling that is totally priceless. I invite you fully to go there. What is the worst that could happen? Life will be lived passionately and abundance opens itself up to you with far less doubt. You will grow into a beautiful tree, well rooted and with lots of fruits to give to all that come close to you.

- Choose and use words that are positive and loving which open up possibilities for you. Ask questions that will help you and others get aware, come alive to do, create, love and get back to your genuine courageous self.

- Create pictures, movies and sound that help move you away from fear and worry. Do your list frequently that gets you back to you. Update your list frequently like your "to-do list".

- List all the things that you love to do, all the things that bring you joy and peace. On another piece of paper write down things that you do that do not bring you joy and peace in order to bring to the surface the behaviours and patterns. Keep those papers with you, so that you can add and subtract to them as you see fit. Slowly, on a day-to-day basis, work toward obtaining and participating in the things that bring you joy and peace. Make a conscious move toward letting go of the things that do not bring you any blessing, joy or peace. This must always be a conscious thing. It takes no time and the benefits are huge!

- Get aware of your body daily, simply by doing meditation or any body awareness technique. Breathe and close your eyes in the morning and at night for just 2 to 5 minutes to start with. Be aware of your face, head, neck, shoulders, chest, arms, stomach,

Be Surprised

legs, and feet and so on, basically all your body parts and breathe deeply. This is one of the simplest healing techniques to get back to yourself and get you resourceful and connected with the genuine you, your spirit or soul. You will also hear your inner voice more. The more you do this exercise, the less you will need to soul search.

- Remember that procrastination will eventually cost you pain, so best to snap out of it earlier! And please remember that just because you are not tuned into the stream of "wow" possibilities, does not mean the channels do not exist!

- Please, remember that nothing you have is truly yours. So, do not make your whole life about acquiring things, as you will have to give it all away sooner or later! Make sure you get to know the joy, blessings and peace in your life before your time is up. It comes sooner than one thinks.

- Remember and know that our truth will always reveal itself to us on our journey. Ask questions and search for your truth, it will come easier.

- What one does consistently is what shapes and make up our life: *"The beginning of a habit is like an incredible threat, but every time we repeat the act we strengthen the strand, add to it another filament, until it becomes a great cable and binds us irrevocably, thought and act."* Orison Swett Marden

- Remember that one must do what one's heart speaks aloud, until one's destiny is truly revealed along the way, rarely before!

- Procrastination equals putting off one's pain or loss and not acting now. So, if one truly looks at it fully and sees the sign of pain to come, it can really shift one to decide more firmly to act and do what must be done now, rarely later! There are always consequences to our decisions.

- Become aware of your actions towards pain or pleasure. Observe frequently what happens without judgement, blame nor analysis.

- Look at the pictures, movies and sounds linked to your pain or pleasure. This will help you quickly get to know how you are wired up. Always listen with your full body, not just your head and always think with your full body (your senses and all your intelligence), not just with your head. That is where all your own secrets wait for you, guaranteed!

- A plan at best is a brilliant guide, as plans always change. Get flexible with it and firm up your commitment by having bigger reasons for your actions towards your heart-felt must-dos. Motivation is never enough. Build your backbone firmly and move away from your wishbone, which takes one nowhere fast.

- Most of the time our mind loses us. But we have not lost our minds! So always use a better source of reference - your heart, your full senses. If you are not there yet then breathe deeply, ask sincere heartfelt questions and wait for your inner guide. It will come and it gets better in a short time, the more you practise!

- **Remember that being great is never about being better than everyone else. It is about being better than who you used to be, the good old you!**

- **Grow to be better than who you used to be, not someone else. This will get you to know your genuine self. This gives you true inner power, natural confidence and self-trust without the constant doubting!**

- **Always be an instrument of peace and genuine love.**

Deciding and the power of decisions

Firstly, decide what you want or deeply desire to happen!

1. When you decide on something, immediately take action on it otherwise you really have not decided "no thing"!

2. Just decide. Do something and never take too long. Time is rarely your best friend. It is around with or without you.

3. Make decisions often. So, you build your muscles for it, a firm backbone and far less wishbone.

4. **Learn from your experience, without judgement, blame nor analysis. Yes, just learn and move on! Do not beat yourself up about it, forgive yourself and others, so you release some space in your head to create more and get conscious to create and do more.**

5. Always remember to breathe deeply when deciding anything, as it accesses your full thinking body, for your best truthful relevant decisions.

6. **Never get stuck or too focused on your results, get flexible again and again… until it clicks.**

7. Enjoy making decisions, play with it again and again! Make it fun!

"When you are inspired by some great purpose, some extraordinary project all your thoughts break their bonds; Your mind transcends limitations, your consciousness expands in every direction, and you find yourself in a new, great and wonderful world. Dormant forces, faculties, talents become alive, and you discover yourself to be a greater person by far than you ever dreamed yourself to be."
Patanjali

"Things turn out best for the people who make the best out of the way things turn out."
Art Linkletter

"The great aim of education is not knowledge but action."
Herbert Spencer

CHAPTER 15

THE FINAL ANALYSIS – MY CONSTANT REMINDER!

We can all find a clear reminder that consistently works for us. I have decided to share mine with you, so you can add it to yours or, of course, find your own. It always moves me to my inner greatness and peace.

It is called The Final Analysis by Mother Theresa.

People are often unreasonable, irrational, and self-centered. Forgive them anyway.

If you are kind, people may accuse you of selfish, ulterior motives. Be kind anyway.

If you are successful, you will win some unfaithful friends and some genuine enemies. Succeed anyway.

If you are honest and sincere, people may deceive you. Be honest and sincere anyway.

What you spend years creating, others could destroy overnight. Create anyway.

If you find serenity and happiness, some may be jealous. Be happy anyway.

The good you do today will often be forgotten. Do good anyway.

Give the best you have, and it will never be enough. Give your best anyway.

In the final analysis, it is between you and God. It was never between you and them anyway.

The power of silence

I am sitting in Glastonbury overlooking the most amazing landscape. All I have is silence and the sound of the birds, the movement and the dance of the trees, the cows making their way in the pasture. I remember the importance of words and sounds and I remember the powerful sensation of no sound.

I wanted to write this chapter about word and how words affect us. The words we hear in our head or from the outside can influence how we feel, influencing our health, our physical state and our wellbeing. These words and thoughts will spin around in our head and, if we are not aware of the chatter, will spin us off further from ourselves. But when we quieten the chatter, it calls us back to our genuine self and we feel surprisingly calmer purely from silence and the lack of sound. How much do we underestimate this and why is it so important to frequently have silence in our lives? We rarely get to experience it, which is why we get the "wow" factor when we are in the presence of beauty or silence or something that brings us back to ourselves.

It has been said time and time again that most human problems and hate in the world are due to our inability to sit quietly, even

for short periods of time. Try sitting with no distractions, with one's back straight, breathing deeply consciously, and thoughtless for an hour a day. If that is too tough or too much of a shock, build up from 10 minutes. The most silent time most people have is during sleep (despite dreams) or just after sex.

Fewer words, more sense!

Words make up about 7% of how we really communicate. We use this 7% to describe something and/or make decisions. However, to communicate fully, engaging all our senses, we have to put more effort into it. For the receiving person to fully understand, we need to explain things in pictures, movies, sounds, touch etc…

When we put words together to explain things, the reader or the listener has an idea, and it is just an idea, or an image, of what we are trying to say. Most of the time when we communicate, we do not really make that much effort with words. Since we use words everyday all day, it is important to understand the impact of words. When we are communicating or listening to words, it is important to use and also engage all our senses, not just our logical mind. This will mean our genuine self will respond, not react. We must be in the right state to be able to respond (which means without blame, judgement or analysis). In our past, instead of speaking one's genuine truth, we left so many things unsaid and leave trails of unnecessary suffering. The unsaid things never really disappear they are badly held in causing pain that is bound to come out somehow because we have waited too long to say what needs saying.

We need to be aware of the words we use. We need to be aware of the words we say to ourselves. We need to be aware that it is an idea, it is an image, it is an imagination and it is not real. Its just words, Remember that others may see it in their heads differently. Most importantly, speak your held in truth earlier particularly if it is really burning you up inside. You will only cause yourself damage or sickness by holding it in. Know that being in the

moment while engaging all your senses is the key. This lights us up much more with our own self-guide.

It is magnificent. It is the first morning in Glastonbury and I am looking at the colourful landscape on my right and on my left. I can hear the breeze and feel it softly caressing my face, as if to say good morning. I can see the movement and hear the sounds of the cows. I can see the birds flying and floating while balancing in the wind. I can see the landscape stretched out in front of me for miles. I can see the mountains in the distance. I can feel the warm sunrays on my skin. It is a beautiful feeling of warmth and love. But this is as far as I can explain with words. When I am here, standing here, what I feel is tremendous. It is true what they say 'a map is never the territory'. Talking about a place is not the same as being there. The words are truly insignificant compared to experiencing that moment. The words fail to describe the experience. So, we must not try and predict the future with our words in our heads and with people. It is best we experience it from now.

Check if what you are thinking is true or not by using certain questions, particularly if your gut contradicts what you are saying out loud. You know the feeling you get in your gut, when your "buddy" disagrees with what you are thinking, a kind of double message that comes about from your body and thoughts almost at the same time, we all get it! You need to ask questions if you have a nudge in your stomach. It makes you feel uncomfortable when in conflict with your mind. It means you need to check your words with your genuine truth because your body knows you better than your thinking or head dialogue.

When you are aware of your true self and what is really around you then you will still hear your head. It talks to you all the time, like a little troubled child that needs attention and must be listened to, so you are totally distracted! When you are using words, breathe and engage your other senses as well. This is the basis of deciding, or feeling, or experiencing anything in the moment - not just on words. Deciding just on words will probably lead you towards fear,

Be Surprised

what you are against rather than for, or something you doubt. It is usually about what you lack. It is important to bring awareness, by engaging all our senses then you will have directness and clarity without the bullshit.

I just want to make clear the enormous importance of checking and observing our words but also as the importance of having no sound. Silence will allow clarity to come to you with more ease, as we are less full.

"Remember that you cannot fill up a cup that is already full".
The Zen Master (Avatar).

We realise the importance of something when we do not have it. Only when I experienced no sound or words, did I realise the importance of not having them! I realised that you can sense more, feel more and be more aware. We do not have to try so hard to engage our feelings. We do not have to try so hard to be aware because we get back to our strength and we get back our energy from having no sound and no words. The chatterbox will slow down and our mind will quieten.

I am sure for many people you will believe the opposite. Silence drives you nuts; it makes you feel very paranoid, it makes you anxious. You are so used to hearing sounds in your head all the time or around you, they take control of you without you even realising. Now, when there is no sound, you might lose control, your mind might lose control, it might lose its hold on you. This feels uncomfortable at first but it will pass. You just never have been there before so your mind is spinning off course, trying to get a grip on you, so your ego can take over, so the genuine you will be hidden in the shadows again.

That is all that is happening, it is nothing to be afraid of. After a while it will pass. Then all the other senses, that you have forgotten how to use, will kick in. Then you will connect back with yourself again, and then you can be more resourceful and

do the things you are supposed to do purposefully, efficiently and without doubt! You can operate on a higher frequency, on a higher energy without much effort. That is the beauty of lack of sound and not listening to the words in your head too much. You can harmonise and go within and find out your own truth and make things happen for you.

As I stand in Glastonbury, looking at this amazing view, the sun coming up, I realise that in order to use words really effectively and efficiently, I have to engage how I feel. The words and thoughts come from inside out, not just from the head, but also from all our senses. For me to write what I have written, I don't think about the words, they just came out based on how I'm feeling, what I'm sensing, what I'm smelling and what's going on. It gives all those words authenticity and that is the power of words when you engage all your senses. Words without engaging all your senses lack complete truth and awareness.

Words are powerful and it is important to know where we go with them. Where is our focus? Do we choose genuine helpful, uplifting words or do we like to stew on words that make our heads spin, judge and analyze? We have all had the experience of someone saying something to us that makes us mad or upset. Yet, the person probably never meant anything like what we thought. It just woke up repressed, bad memories linked to our past history. It is those unsaid or unexpressed past thoughts catching up with you!

Influencing our self to make a difficult change!

If you were selling yourself to you, what would you say about you? Write it down…

If you do not know who you are, why would anyone else be drawn to you? So, do not hold back on this, it is important to see one's true self and gifted qualities. Write a list of your qualities and revisit it every day to strengthen your roots. What would you say about you that would make you have confidence, courage, and trust and to believe in yourself? Do this in a fun way... remember no analysis, blame or judgement.

Your Genuine Needs and Musts!

What is a must for you? What do you feel you need the most? Write it down or record it. What would make you curious about you if you just met yourself? It may seem strange but we do this to others when we meet them, we get attracted to others for these simple notions. We often think the worst of ourselves most of the time. So, it is important to carry on...

What do you feel you deeply want?

Again, write it down or record it. Just guess no pressure, remember no blame, judgement or analysis!

What do you feel it would really mean to you if you had these things?

What stops you from getting the things you most desire? What don't you like or love about yourself or others?

What do you feel would happen to you, to your business or work if you did not get your desired results? What would that mean to you exactly?

Where are you right now in your life?

What is your frame of reference you focus on? The internal frame of reference that you go to most? Be brutally honest. Basically, what do you think about most of your days?

How do you know when you have done your best for you?

What do you feel must happen exactly for you to know this?

Do you really like getting things done and do you really enjoy the process?

What has to happen for you to believe something is true?

What evidence do you need, see, hear, feel, touch, taste or sense?

How long, time wise, does it take for you to believe something is true?

Do you need to be shown several times before you believe it is true?

This chapter is about influencing yourself, embracing the questions designed for important self-observation that are crucial to knowing yourself.

However, we seem more interested in influencing others. So, we will do both. It just seems easier to focus on others. We simply cannot genuinely influence others if we cannot find ourselves first. People will discover we are frauds eventually as acting or playing a role cannot be carried on forever, at some point the curtain has to come down on the play!

Body Language or Physiology - The unpopular Truth!

How we feel or breathe makes us who we are in that moment. If we physically shrink in any way, we become less resourceful. If we extend our body or stand straight up we radiate at a higher energy and can do great things beyond what we generally believe is possible. It also reduces the mind spinning and moves us away from being strangers to ourselves. We generally live in the shadow most of the time – after all old habits die hard. Or could it be that you feel friends, society or your tribe may not accept your true self? You will find that when you radiate at a higher energy people are naturally drawn to you. This will also affect your tone of voice both internally and externally. When we are in this state, we can find something in common with others, which links us to our true self. We get familiar with ourselves again, just like we get familiar with others. You know the feeling when you feel comfortable with someone like you have been his or her friend or lover for years… and you have only just met him or her.

Another form of communication is our physical or body language. It accounts for around 55% of our communication. And 38% is tone - what we sound like, sad or happy, sincere or untrue, cold or warm etc, you get the idea. You say something but the tone sets it apart, either to yourself in your head or to others. This will determine whether they are feeling you or not!

Interestingly, the impact of words makes up just 7% of our communication yet this is where we put all our focus and energy. As we are more comfortable with ourselves, we dive deeper into our internal physiology or instinctive body language. This is the grand dialogue you really want to hear and this naturally comes from your source. Staying with your heart's truth will always stir this up and you will start to hear it more and need to think far less. Your mind will simply follow as your real voice or inner guide will simply not be denied! The thing is how do we stay there, without all the distractions and drama?

Let us ask ourselves, what would happen if I just stayed the same for the next 10 years?

Let us look at this from a different angle and ask, how can you create a demand for your true self? What do you feel must happen for you to want to spend time with the real you, the genuine you? Answer it for you. What would your life be like if you managed your state? What would your career be like by now? **Most people do not succeed because they major their lives with minor things!** What excuses or reasons do you make up to convince yourself to stay in this unhelpful state?

If you find reasons not to do something you know you must, then you need to ask questions and find a way to commit to stretching yourself. Basically, if you think you cannot, then you simply must do it! If you have not got the courage for this then you must find your own ways to steer you into action. **Our goals are not what really drive us to do anything; it is always the reasons behind our goals that make us really do something.**

If you spent 5% of your time thinking about how you achieved something that you never thought you could do, you will not only strengthen your resolve but you will also build up your muscles that allow you to trust yourself and improve your inner courage to do more bigger challenges.

We mostly 'hypnotise ourselves' by constantly repeating unhelpful words in our heads which reduce our energy and make us less of a person. It is important to choose your words wisely so that you feel good. You need to make it a new daily habit, just like brushing your teeth. It is best to do something every day to recondition and hypnotise ourselves to succeed, if not someone else will recondition us or hypnotise us for their own success! We can see this in the companies we work for, the press, the shops, the TV adverts for things we don't really need, or people that want something from us for their own benefit. This only happens because our mind is weak and we are not in charge of it, it is in charge of us.

How did you convince yourself do things historically? Again, make a list, and, if your mind answers I do not know - well you know the drill - just guess, no pressure, no analysis, and no judgement. Go for it and when your list stops, just ask, what else do I feel? Just think back and keep writing.

What were the logical reasons that helped you get into action for your own benefit?

What were your logical reasons that helped you get into action for other people's benefit? Even when we are doing something for others, we are still getting something from it.

A Little Recap

Breathe consciously. Make sure you do not restrict your breathing by shrinking your body or having thoughts that shorten your breath and stiffen your body. Restrictive, unconscious breathing is what we do regularly without realizing. Our body only breathes for us properly when we sleep. Half breathing or short, shallow breathing means we are running at half capacity both physically and mentally. Automatically we worry when we are limited in breath, so we lose focus and go to our fears. It is so vital to observe your physical state and your breathing – that way you can win the majority of battles with worry! That way you will get greater clarity and make better decisions without all the constant head spinning.

Worry light if you must. Here is a technique that will reduce worry and anxiety. Sit up straight, breathe deeply and push your belly out (like Buddha Belly) and release the air from your mouth with a shhhh sound loudly to force out the air. Repeat this 20 times and it will remove any anxious feeling in the gut. It will help you to reduce your worries and anxieties and will put you in a more resourceful state. You will also feel good in this moment!

You must feel yourself at all times. This is where the truth lies. When you get a rhythm for feeling yourself then all things will get so much easier. When you surrender to your inner guide, your truth, everything becomes possible. You lose your fear, and once you lose your fear, you completely lose your doubts. Oh, what a marvellous feeling it is, the ultimate freedom to do anything. It truly means everything is possible from then onwards. Your life literally begins and then you can breathe again.

One of my very close soul mates friend said that after a year of hell full of problems, fears and challenges, she moved towards self-awareness, clarity and growth, making her more at peace with herself. In that year it did not just rain, it poured on her! At the age of 34, Karin got cancer and also experienced several personal traumas. Karin's approach to healing herself was through the support of close friends, holistic alternative therapists and myself. Karin's cancer was cured without the aid of chemotherapy and other medical drugs. After her hard-core journey to full recovery, Karin said this:

"Had I known this before, I would not have been so worried!"
Dr Karin Mairhofer

Motion: meaning changing your body position regularly to feel good. Check your physiology often so you build up far less doubt.

Remember the words of Albert Einstein *"nothing changes unless something first moves!"*

Check your thinking if your gut reacts - it is double messaging!

Action what you must do, frequently. If you think you cannot it usually means you must, so find a bigger reason for doing it! It will build your backbone much more and not your "wishbone".

Remember that doing what you must now and today means you do not have to worry about it tomorrow.

Service your body regularly. Treat it at least like you would your car! This is much cheaper than leaving it until major work is needed.

Who are you now? Who do you choose to become in the future from now? Are you genuinely true to yourself most of the time? And if so, who are you becoming? Who do you 'heart-fully' choose to become in the future? No more holding back, living in the shadow!

Smile genuinely and regularly! It is important to have laughter in your life daily. Laughter is like having a shot of vitamin B12. It elevates your mood and makes you feel good. When you smile or laugh, it is contagious and the people around you are affected in a positive way. It also eases tension. If you are in a good mood and you expect others to be in a good mood, the likelihood is much higher because you set your intentions to be in that state of mind. So, things happen more smoothly for you, with far less effort.

CHAPTER 16

INSPIRING STORIES AND CLEAR INSIGHTS!

Addiction

"I share this example simply to illustrate that little by little I kept experiencing more repercussions from my drinking problem. I knew that drinking and driving was not good for me, but I kept doing it. I knew that when I drank, I drank too much, but I kept doing it. I kept turning the volume higher and higher, until I had to listen. Life was kind and I was kind. I gave myself opportunities to learn my lesson the best way I knew how. As I was unwilling to learn this lesson, I gave myself more pronounced opportunities in order to finally learn what I was trying to teach myself. And just when my ears started to hurt enough, I decided to learn my lesson. All these opportunities were, in actuality, gifts to myself. Gifts of growth, the DWAI, the blackouts, the crash, the allergic reactions, all helped me learn my lesson. Most people would perceive the DWAI (Driving While Ability Impaired) as bad luck, others would perceive the crash as an accident, but to me, all those situations were in the end, gifts I offered myself. The police officer was kind enough to give of his time to assist me in my growth, and I now smile every time I carefully and respectfully pass the tree outside the synagogue."

James Blanchard Cisneros

"To illustrate the seriousness of drinking, we now know that Jellinek's disease (alcoholism) is responsible for:

- 50 percent of all auto fatalities
- 80 percent of all domestic violence/abuse
- 30 percent of all suicides
- 60 percent of all child abuse
- 65 percent of all drowning
- It is estimated that when a woman contracts the disease, her husband leaves her in nine out of ten cases. When a man contracts it, his wife leaves in one out of ten cases." Kathleen W. Fitzgerald

The following is a personal story sent in to James Blanchard Cisneros by a person from Canada, who wishes to remain anonymous.

Hello,

There is so much I'd like to say, but the best place to start is by saying Thank You. I'd like to tell you a story that happened and tell you why I'm grateful, but I would also like to remain anonymous, if that's ok. After quitting high school at 15, I spent 20 years in the working world, from being a soldier to eventually having my own technology firms, and then finally as an up-and-coming executive hopeful in the world's biggest technology studio.

I didn't know then that so much of what I did was ruled by ego. I was good at everything I did in the workplace, but lousy at relationships; I didn't know that I had a deep pain that needed healing. Despite being a corporate star and loving the glory, I really loathed the work as I felt like I was missing the point of being alive.

In 2006, I discovered that my relationship was based on deceit, and my partner encouraged me to use drugs; this was a pre-meditated plan that had been in the works for two years. I later found out that I was a target for a group of con artists headed by my ex, whose methods were to finish off their marks by getting them into narcotics, thereby isolating the mark from their friends, and also using the addiction as a way to eliminate the mark's credibility with police so that their accusers would only be seen as drug-crazed loonies. It all sounds pretty whack, even to write about it now - it was so far from what I thought was even remotely possible.

Even more so was that in late 2006, all of this culminated in my being on the street as a homeless drug addict with a questionable state of mental health and countless attempts at suicide. It was a long way from the executive floor where I worked just four short months before. I was perhaps thirty minutes away from an intentional final overdose and driving a car into the ocean when my brother found me. He had flown across the country and had been walking the streets of the west coast city I lived in for a week looking for me.

I was very confused when I came home; due both to the detoxing, and to the pain and anger at my ex-girlfriend's actions to the abandonment of my friends in what was my greatest hour of need. At the time, I didn't see any of it for the gift that it was. After I came home, an angel practitioner told me that all of these experiences were meant to bring me back from the west coast, and start a new career helping people by creating a new program for treating people with addictions. I didn't believe it; by this time, I'd also lost all faith that God existed. But she also told me that God and angels intervened directly to ensure that I didn't die, as I've got too important a mission here, and that it's time I was on the path to spiritual discovery. I only half believed that. The ego wanted to do things its way.

In the past year and half, I have experienced things I never knew were possible: joy, God, Well-Being...so much that I'm overwhelmed with the feeling of love from God and the universe. The road to here has been rocky, with periods of immense joy and other times of immense desperation and depression; those latter times are when I felt that God was abandoning me during my spiritual enlightenment. Periodically, over the same period since coming home, I lost faith in people and shut myself away from the world.

It was during one of these times that a friend pointed me to your site, and to your book.

I'm 36 now, living with my Mom and studying psychology at university, while figuring out that God has perfect timing for what he wants me to do. I wanted to say thank you because you sent me your book and I couldn't afford to buy it. When it arrived, I realized what it means to walk one's talk, and you helped to restore my faith in humanity. For that I will be eternally grateful. One day I hope to repay your kindness in a way that spreads love and light. I can't entirely say why I went through the experiences I did, but I do know now that I set up all of these lessons as a learning experience at some level that I am not fully aware of. There is so much to learn! Thank you, thank you, and thank you.
Anonymous

Anger

"Anger. It's a peculiar yet predictable emotion. It begins as a drop of water. An irritant. A frustration. Nothing big, just an aggravation. Someone gets your parking place. Someone pulls in front of you on the freeway. A waitress is slow and you are in a hurry. The toast burns. Drops of water. Drip. Drip. Drip. Drip. Yet, enough of these seemingly innocent drops of anger and before long you've got a bucket full of rage. Walking revenge. Blind bitterness. Unharnessed hatred. We trust no one and bare our teeth at anyone who gets near. We become walking time bombs that, given just the right tension and fear, could explode.

Now, is that any way to live? What good has hatred ever brought? What hope has anger ever created? What problems have ever been resolved by revenge?"
Max Lucado, No Wonder They Call Him Saviour

"There is a difference between speaking with anger and speaking your truth. When you speak with anger, know that the ego-self is speaking. Know that you're reacting to and focusing on an illusion you see as real. When you speak with anger you bring forth knowingly or not, emotionally repressed feelings from the past. You replace the present with the past and you lose the *opportunity to experience what is really going on. When you speak with anger, you are not really concerned with how those listening to you will feel. All you really care about is that your point of view is heard. When you come from such a place, all you are doing is making the listener defensive. The listener then puts up a wall to defend himself or herself against the perceived attack."*

"As a result, you end up arguing or shouting at a wall with the hopes of being heard. Regardless of how smart or right you believe yourself to be, you will not be heard by a wall. Obviously, a wall is not a good listener, which creates frustration. The frustration leads to confusion, which then ends in regret. This person, knowing that he cannot communicate with you, will move on to someone he believes will listen to what you did to him. This creates more frustration and miscommunication on everyone's part. In short, whenever you speak with anger, regardless of whether or not you believe you have every right to do so, frustration, confusion, separation and regret are your end result."

"When you react unconstructively, your emotion is that of anger. You become angered by others' actions, which because of their immature nature, they had little control over. Your anger now becomes an immature reaction to their immature action. So ask yourself, where does this leave the two of you? Definitely not in a peaceful place! This peaceful place is found by reacting with compassion and love toward your brother or sister. This peaceful place can be your goal in every situation. This peaceful place is your natural state, and your natural state is not temporal in nature. Reacting with anger and condemnation might bring you a false and very temporary state of peace from the simple misperception that you are right and they are wrong, and that the wrong deserves to be punished. Remember your ego always answers first, and its primary goal is for you to separate from your brother or sister. Ask yourself: Would I rather be right or happy? Would I rather express false power or experience everlasting peace?"

"The ego has taught you that if someone cuts you off in traffic, you should react with emotions such as annoyance, irritation, anger, or rage. The world considers any of these emotions to be natural and deserved responses. The world tells you that you have every right to be angry. It feels natural and right to react with anger because that is how you have been trained and what you are now used to. In fact, you probably consider what is natural

and what you're used to as basically the same thing. I offer to you that what you are used to and what is natural more often than not are usually two completely different things. Any time you react with anger, such a reaction occurs not because it is natural, but because it is has become a bad habit. You have learned negative tendencies, have not corrected them and they have now become bad habits that you now call your natural behaviour. **You have repeated these bad habits over a period of time and they have now become "second nature" or natural tendencies. But many of those reactions you consider natural tendencies have, in truth, nothing to do with your true nature**. As a child, your parents, other family members and friends probably reacted this way. As a child this type of reaction was probably common, first with your parents and family members, then with your peers. As adults, they probably still react this way and you have probably joined them in their thinking. At first, such reactions probably did not sit right with you but as you heard your family react over and over in such a manner, sooner or later you got used to the behaviour, and let it be."

"The next time you become angry with another driver, feel what that does to you, not only to your outer self but also to your inner self. Feel the heavy fog roll through your heart, feel its denseness. Feel the tension in your body, the anxiety. Then listen to the sadness in your soul. Hear it for the first time asking you this one simple question: Why would anyone in their right mind do something like this to themselves over and over again? Ask yourself: "What am I doing to myself? What am I accomplishing?" Then, as the fog dissipates and the light begins to shine through, say this: I simply choose not to do this any longer to myself! There is another way I can react! I will choose to see God's child in my brother and sister!"

"The only value these behaviours hold for you and the world is for you to recognize them for what they are to you and the world: your unnatural self, your false self, your ego-self. The only value they hold for you and the world is to experience them for a long enough period of time for you to get physically, mentally and spiritually sick of them. When you've had enough of them you will get to the point where you will no longer choose or want to live this way. You will no longer choose to support them and torture yourself. You will no longer choose to support them and torture others."
James Blanchard Cisneros

Attitude and Mind State

"We who lived in the concentration camps can remember the men who walked through the huts comforting others, giving away their last piece of bread. They may have been few in number, but they offer sufficient proof that everything can be taken from a man but one thing: The last of his freedoms - to choose one's attitude in any given set of circumstances, to choose one's own way."
Victor E. Frankl, Man's Search for Meaning

"Jerry was always in a good mood, and always had something positive to say. When someone would ask him how he was doing, he would reply, "If I were any better, I would be twins!" He was a unique manager because he had several waiters who had followed him around from restaurant to restaurant. The reason the waiters followed Jerry was his attitude. He was a natural motivator. If an employee was having a bad day, Jerry was there, telling the employee how to look on the positive side of the situation."

"Seeing this style really made me curious, so one day I approached Jerry and remarked, "I don't get it! You can't be a positive person all of the time. How do you do it?"

Jerry replied, "Each morning, I wake up and say to myself, 'Jerry, you have two choices today. You can choose to be in a good mood or you can choose to be in a bad mood.' I choose to be in a good mood. Each time something bad happens, I can choose to be a victim or I can choose to learn from it. I choose to learn from it. Every time someone comes to me complaining, I can choose to accept his complaining or I can point out the positive side of life. I choose the positive side of life."

"Yeah, right, it's not that easy," I protested.

"Yes, it is," Jerry said. "Life is all about choices. When you cut away all the junk, every situation is a choice. You choose how you react to situations. You choose how people will affect your mood. You choose to be in a good mood or bad mood. The bottom line: It's your choice how you live life."

"I reflected on what Jerry said. Soon thereafter, I left the restaurant industry to start my own business. We lost touch, but I often thought about him when I made a choice about life instead of reacting to it. Several years later, I heard that Jerry did something you are never supposed to do in a restaurant business; he left the back door open one morning and was held up at gun point by three armed robbers. While trying to open the safe, his hand, shaking from nervousness, slipped off the combination. The robbers panicked and shot him. Luckily, Jerry was found relatively quickly and rushed to the local trauma centre. After 18 hours of surgery and weeks of intensive care, Jerry was released from the hospital with fragments of the bullets still in his body.

I saw Jerry about six months after the accident. When I asked him how he was, he said, "If I were any better, I'd be twins. Wanna see my scars?" I declined to see his wounds but did ask him what had gone through his mind as the robbery took place.

"The first thing that went through my mind was that I should have locked the back door," Jerry replied. "Then, as I lay on the floor, I remembered that I had two choices: I could choose to live, or I could choose to die. I chose to live."

"Weren't you scared? Did you lose consciousness?" I asked.

Jerry continued, "The paramedics were great. They kept telling me I was going to be fine. But when they wheeled me into the emergency room and I saw the expressions on the faces of the doctors and nurses, I got really scared. In their eyes, I read, 'He's a dead man.' I knew I needed to take action."

"What did you do?" I asked. "Well, there was a big, burly nurse shouting questions at me," said Jerry. "She asked if I was allergic to anything. "Yes," I replied. The doctors and nurses stopped working as they waited for my reply. I took a deep breath and yelled, "Bullets!" Over their laughter, I told them, "I am choosing to live. Operate on me as if I am alive, not dead."

Jerry lived, thanks to the skill of his doctors, but also because of his amazing

attitude. I learned from him that every day we have the choice to live fully. Attitude, after all, is everything."
Anonymous

Jerry lived his life with courage and self-trust, made constantly from the heart with choice at all cost. His story was and will always be an inspiration to many.

Here Now or Getting Lost Constantly!

"My friend, if you're not in the now, you are lost. You call a foreign place home and wonder why you feel lost and alone. You bring judgments of the past into the present and question why you don't understand what is really going on. You look at a brother or sister, call him or her a stranger instead of a friend and speculate as to why you live in fear. My friend, you live in fear because you bring all your past judgments into the present moment. You extend your past into your present, creating a future like your past, and thus you never really experience the present. Living this way, you will never experience the perfection of the present moment.

The present is your God's eternal gift to you. It is when you look at a brother or sister without past judgments and see a friend. When you see your brother or sister as your God's perfect creation, you are experiencing the present moment. It happens when you look into your brother or sister's eyes and see yourself reflected in them. You need only do this once and you will want no other way. If you see your brother or sister as something other than your God's perfect creation, know that you are exchanging your past judgments for the present moment."
James Blanchard Cisneros

Challenges

"An old man and his son worked a small farm, with only one horse to pull the plow. One day, the horse ran away.

"How terrible," sympathized the neighbours " What bad luck."

"Who knows whether it is bad luck or good luck," the farmer replied.

A week later, the horse returned from the mountains, leading five wild mares into the barn.

"What wonderful luck!" said the neighbours.

"Good luck? Bad luck? Who knows?" answered the old man.

The next day, the son, trying to tame one of the horses, fell and broke his leg.

"How terrible. What bad luck!" "Bad luck? Good Luck?"

The army came to all the farms to take the young men for war, but the farmer's son was of no use to them, so he was spared. "Good? Bad?"
Dan Millman, Way of the Peaceful Warrior

"Today, when I awoke, I suddenly realized that this is the best day of my life, ever!" There were times when I wondered if I would make it to today; but I did! And because I did, I'm going to celebrate! Today I'm going to celebrate what an unbelievable life I have had so far; the accomplishments, the many blessings, and yes, even the hardships, because they have served to make me stronger. I will live this day with my head held high and a happy heart. I will take time to marvel at God's seemingly simple gifts, the morning dew, the sun, the clouds, the trees, the flowers, and the birds."

"Today, none of these miraculous creations will escape my notice. Today I will share my excitement for life with other people. I'll make someone smile. I'll go out of my way to perform an act of kindness for someone I don't even know."

"Today I'll give a word of encouragement to someone who seems down. I'll pay someone a sincere compliment. I'll tell a child how special they are. And I'll tell someone I love, just how deeply I care for them and how much they mean to me."

"Today is the day I quit worrying about what I don't have, and start

being grateful for all the wonderful things God has already given me. I'll remember that to worry is just a waste of time, because my faith in God and His divine plan ensures everything will be just fine. And tonight, before I go to bed, I'll take a stroll outside and raise my eyes to the heavens. I will stand in awe at the beauty of the stars and the moon and the majesty of the universe and I will praise God for these magnificent treasures. As the day ends and I lay my head down, I will thank the Almighty for the best day of my life. And I will sleep the sleep of a contented child, and yet excited with expectation, because I know tomorrow is going to be the best day of my life, ever!"
Gregory M. Lousig-Nont, PhD, The Best Day of my Life

"I asked God for strength, that I might achieve. I was made weak that I might learn humbly to obey, and see clearer...
I asked for health, that I might do great things. I was given infirmity, that I might do better things...
I asked for riches, that I might be happy. I was given poverty, that I might be wise...
I asked for power, that I might have the praise of men. I was given weakness, that I might feel the need of God and empathy towards others...
I asked for all things, that I might enjoy life. I was given life, that I may enjoy all things... I got nothing I asked for-but everything I had hoped for. Almost despite myself, my unspoken prayers were answered. I am among men, most richly blessed, I pray I remember daily!"
An unknown confederate soldier, a creed for those who have suffered.

In his book, *Something's Going on Here,* Bob Benson offers another example of how an individual can completely change his or her thoughts and attitude about an event in one's life by simply reinterpreting the event in one's mind. Bob writes:

"W.T., how did you like your heart attack?"
"It scared me to death, almost."
"Would you like to do it again?"
"No!"
"Would you recommend it?"

"Definitely not."
"Does your life mean more to you than it did before?"
"Well, yes."
"You and Nell have always had a beautiful marriage, but now are you closer than ever?"
"Yes."
"How about that new granddaughter?" "
Yes. Did I show you her picture?"
"Do you have a new compassion for people a deep understanding and sympathy?" "Yes."
"Do you know the Lord in a richer, deeper fellowship than you had ever realized could be possible?"
"Yes."
"How did you like your heart attack?"
Silence was his answer.
Bob Benson, *Something's Going on Here*

Children

"We have not inherited the earth from our fathers but are borrowing it from our children."
Native American proverb

"Your children are not your children. They are the sons and daughters of life's longing for itself. They come through you but not from you, and though they are with you, yet they belong not to you. You may give them your love but not your thoughts, for they have their own thoughts. You may house their bodies but not their souls, for their souls dwell in the house of tomorrow, which you cannot visit, not even in your dreams. You may strive to be like them, but seek not to make them like you, for life goes not backward nor tarries with yesterday. You are the bows from which your children as Living arrows are sent forth. The archer sees the mark upon the path of the infinite, and He bends you with His might that His arrows might go swift and far. Let your bending in the archer's hand be for gladness; For even as He loves the arrow that flies, So He loves also the bow that is stable."
Kahill Gibran

Making choices, creating and always finding a way!

"Going to a junkyard is a sobering experience. There you can see the ultimate destination of almost everything we desired."
Roger Von Oech, A Wack on the Side of the Head

"When you were born, you cried and the world rejoiced. Live your life in such a manner that when you die, the world cries and you rejoice."
Indian proverb

Remember... "if you have a lemon, make a lemonade".
The late Julius Rosenwald, President of Sears, Roebuck & Co.

Here is an interesting, stimulating short story by Thelma Thompson: " During the War, my husband was stationed at an Army training camp near the Mojave Desert, in California. I went to live there in order to be near him. I hated the place. I loathed it. I had never before been so miserable. My husband was ordered out on manoeuvres in the Mojave Deserts, and I was left in a tiny shack alone. The heat was unbearable – 125 degrees in the shade of a cactus. Not a soul to talk to. The wind blew incessantly, and all the food I ate, and the very air I breathed, were filled with sand, sand!"

"I was so utterly wretched, so sorry for myself that I wrote to my parents. I told them I was giving up and coming back home. I said I couldn't stand it one minute longer. I would rather be in jail! My father answered my letter with just two lines – two lines that will always sing in my memory – two lines that completely altered my life:

"Two men looked out from prison bars. One saw the mud, the other saw the stars."

"I read those two lines over, and over. I was ashamed of myself. I made up my mind I would find out what was good in my present situation; I would look for the stars."

"I made friends with the natives, and their reaction amazed me. When I showed interest in their weaving and pottery, they gave me presents of

their favourite pieces, which they refused to sell to tourists. I studied the fascinating forms of the cactus, and the yuccas and the Joshua trees. I learned about prairie dogs, watched for the desert sunsets, and hunted for seashells that had been on the ocean floor."

"What brought this astonishing change in me? The Mojave Desert hadn't changed. But I had. I had changed my attitude of mind. And by doing so, I transformed a wretched experience into the most exciting adventure of my life. I was stimulated and excited by this new world that I had discovered. I was so excited I wrote a book about it – a novel that was published under the title "Bright Ramparts"… I had looked out of my self-created prison and found the stars…!"
Thelma Thompson

Thelma Thompson discovered an old Greek saying from as far back as 500BC *"The best things are the most difficult"*. So get to love challenges and dance with them and if you can't dance, breathe with it calmly, while smiling and then go from there!

Harry Emerson Fosdick repeated it in the 21st century saying: *"Happiness is not mostly pleasure; it is mostly victory"*.

Remember your victories that come from a sense of achievement, a sense of triumph, from turning your lemons into lemonades… they will always serve you well like they did others and me. This is a certainty!

The poet Douglas Malloch also put it clearly and simply:

"If you can't be a pine on the top of the hill,
Be a scrub in the valley – but be
The best little scrub by the side of the rill;
Be a bush, if you can't be a tree.

If you can't be a bush, be a bit of the grass,
And some highway happier make;
If you can't be a musky, then just be a bass –
But the liveliest bass in the lake!

We can't all be captains; we've got to be crew,
There's big work to do and there's lesser to do
And the task we must do is the near.

If you can't be a highway, then just be trail,
If you can't be the sun, be the star;
It isn't by size that you win or you fail –
Be the best of whatever you are!"

Douglas Malloch

Let's not imitate others for long, let's genuinely find us and be ourselves… through our heart-felt choices!

"Trials are but lessons that you failed to learn presented once again, so where you made a faulty choice before, you can now make a better one, and thus escape all the pain that your previous choices brought to you."
A Course in Miracles

Compassion Always

"Compassion is not quantitative. Certainly it is true that behind every human being who cries out for help there may be a million or more equally entitled to attention. But this is the poorest of all reasons for not helping the person whose cries you hear. Where, then, does one begin or stop? How to choose? How to determine which one of a million sounds surrounding you is more deserving than the rest? Do not concern yourself in such speculations. You will never know; you will never need to know. Reach out and take hold of the one who happens to be nearest. If you are never able to help or save another, at least you will have saved one. To help put meaning into a single life may not produce universal regeneration, but it happens to represent the basic form of energy in a society. It also is the test of individual responsibility."
Norman Cousins, Human Options

Death Fully Awake

Joseph Bayly wrote the following extract, after he laid three of his sons to rest. It may give you some insight on how to comfort loved ones as they grieve.

"I was sitting, torn by grief. Someone came and talked to me of God's dealings, of why it happened, of hope beyond the grave. He talked constantly; he said things I knew were true. I was unmoved except to wish he'd go away. He finally did. Another came and sat beside me. He just sat beside me for an hour and more, listened when I said something, answered briefly, prayed simply, left. I was moved. I was comforted. I hated to see him go."
Joseph Bayly, *Act of Love*

On Dying Young

"An individual dies young because he has completed his task. The being that has passed will be reminded of his task and that it was indeed his time. He will be offered a glance of the future of all those left behind, and he will find comfort and peace in this. You are an eternal being. Your brother is an eternal being. Once you leave this earth, this so-called young soul becomes a very old soul."
Pat Rodegast, *Emmanuel*

On Preparing for the Loss of Loved Ones

"There are two answers. Loved ones are never lost. You must experience it in your own way. Of course, you will miss the physical being but when you learn to go beyond that, there will be no missing at all. Even as you sit in your human form, once you allow yourself-notice the word "allow" to believe that you exist beyond the physical, you will touch hands with those who have left. And it will be real. It will be more real than the physicality that you had touched before. Are you aware that the physical body is a shield or a shell? It does not reveal but rather hinders revelation. If you did not have need of illusion you would not need a physical body at all.

What should you do immediately following the death of a loved one? That is an excellent question. First, the willingness to let that person go to the next step in their evolution is extremely helpful, not only to you but to them. A " farewell," a "bon voyage," a "Godspeed." Then the rest of you look at each other and give comfort and assurance, and provide all the hugs and tissues that are necessary. Next, take yourself to a place of great luxury and enjoy an incredible feast. Salute the soul that has completed its task. Give a toast to the time you will meet again and go about the business of your own lives. Death is not only a time of mourning. It is a time of truth."

"Karmic ties can be formed by an unwillingness to express any negativity thus holding resentments that go into the soul consciousness to return in another life. By your dealing with the negative emotion, by cleansing the relationship, you are helping both of you. The saying "Don't speak ill of the dead," is nonsense. There is no such thing."
Pat Rodegast, *Emmanuel*

Most of us have read or seen television accounts of people who said they 'died' and went through a tunnel towards "the light." The most eloquent way that I have seen this light being described is in the book *A Course in Miracles*. The description is as follows:

"Beyond the body, beyond the sun and stars, past everything you see and yet somehow familiar, is an arc of golden light that stretches as you look into a great and shining circle. And the entire circle fills with light before your eyes. The edges of the circle disappear, and what is in it is no longer contained at all. The light expands and covers everything, extending to infinity, forever shining and with no break or limit anywhere. Within it, everything is joined in perfect continuity. Nor is it possible to imagine that anything could be outside, for there is nowhere that this light is not."
A Course in Miracles

"If you are thinking you might get bored or tired after being in heaven for a while...don't worry! Try to imagine something with me. Imagine you are a little bird who lives in a tiny cage made of rusty metal. And inside your

cage you have a food dish, and a little mirror, and a tiny perch to swing on. Then one day, some kind person takes your cage to a big, beautiful forest. The forest is splashed with sunlight. Proud, towering trees cover the hills and valleys as far as you can see. There are gushing waterfalls, and bushes drooping with purple berries, and fruit trees, and carpets of wild flowers, and a wide blue sky to fly in. And besides all these things, there are millions of other little birds, hopping from one green limb to another and eating their fill, and raising their little families, and singing their hearts out all through the day. Now, little bird, can you imagine wanting to stay in your cage? Can you imagine saying, "Oh please don't let me go. I will miss my cage, I will miss my little food dish with seeds in it. I will miss my plastic mirror and my tiny little perch. I might get bored in that big forest."
Larry Libby, *Someday Heaven*

"If illusions are by definition nothing, then different illusions can only be encountered through your attempt to separate nothingness into parts. Only the delusional mind can see different levels of nothingness as separate and real. You can stack up your hundreds and thousands of personal levels of illusions and still not come close to the height of an atom. Only a delusional mind can believe that it needs to fight through different levels of nothingness, with different levels of answers, to obtain peace. The ego supports the efforts of a delusional mind, for the ego is the father and creator of the delusional mind. And a creator will support his creations. Although there are countless levels of illusions that the ego supports, there are four main illusionary barriers that the average delusional mind passes through in order to find the truth about the subject of giving.

Offer these four, not only because they are the ones I personally had to pass I through, but also because I have seen many of my friends and family members experience them. If you give, you lose. If you give, you must get something of equal or greater physical value in return. If you give, you must at least get something of mental value in return. If you give, all situations must be judged as separate and given separate consideration with regard to getting something or anything in return."
James Blanchard Cisneros

Enlightenment or Simply Awareness

"Life has cycles. Whatever goes up, comes down, and what falls can rise again. Progress can be slow: We remember, then we forget, then we remember; we take two steps forward, then one step back. No matter how enlightened we become, we still face the realities of daily life.

A lesson on enlightenment may be learned from the following anecdote: A young man had spent five arduous years searching for truth. One day, as he walked up into the foothills of a great mountain range, he saw an old man approach from above, walking down the path carrying a heavy sack on his back. He sensed that this old man had been to the mountaintop; he had finally found one of the wise-ones who could answer his heart's deepest questions.

"Please, Sir" he asked. "Tell me the meaning of enlightenment."

The old man smiled, and stopped. Then, fixing his gaze on the youth, he slowly swung the heavy burden off his back, laid the sack down and stood up straight.

"Ah, I understand," the young man replied. "But, Sir, what comes after enlightenment?"

The old man took a deep breath, then swung the heavy sack over his shoulders and continued on his way.

Socrates (character in the story) once told me, "A flash of enlightenment offers a preview of coming attractions, but when it fades, you will see more clearly what separates you from that state your compulsive habits, outmoded beliefs, false associations and other mental structures." Just when our lives are starting to get better, we may feel like things are getting worse because for the first time we see clearly what needs to be done.

"After illumination," Socrates continued, "difficulties continue to arise; what changes is your relationship to them. You see more and resist less.

You gain the capacity to turn your problems into lessons and your lessons into wisdom."
Dan Millman, *No Ordinary Moments*

"Others, and close ones will experience how you act and treat them. They will want to be like you and understand what it is you are doing in your life to be this way. And you will smile, but not from a sense of superiority, but from the knowing that what your brothers and sisters are searching for, they already have. They will think of themselves as spiritual children learning or less, but you will know them as complete equals and peers. They will ask you questions that they believe they do not know the answers to, and yet when you answer them, their memories will be reawakened, and they will simply remember that they already know what you are saying to them. They will understand that the answer had always been within them, simply waiting for the question to be asked. You will remind them that all questions they could ever ask are exactly like that first question they themselves answered. They will recognize great freedom in this. They will recognize this memory as true. They will thank you for helping them remember their true selves and you Will thank them for not letting you forget yours."

"You will experience great joy and fulfillment from your interaction with your brothers and sisters. You will live in joy with the knowledge that all your brothers and sisters are either living in joy or searching for it. You will even love and respect those you perceive, as not searching for joy, for where they are in their remembering has nothing to do with their perfection. You recognize and know them all as the perfect expressions of God, and it makes no difference where they believe themselves to be in that recognition." "And finally, at the fourth level of perception, you acknowledge that there are no such things as "bad things." Gratitude becomes your only response to each and every situation. At this level of thinking, you know with utmost certainty that nothing comes to you that is not held in your mind. If properly perceived, the previous statement offers absolute and total freedom. You understand that you do have the power to determine what will enter your mind. You know that there is no force outside of you that brings lessons that should be experienced as unpleasant. When you are in touch with peace, which is your natural inheritance, you are in a harmonious state.

As a result, you make requests from this state and the results of your experiences will be harmonious and peaceful."
James Blanchard Cisneros

Continuous Forgiveness…

"It was at a church in Munich that I saw him, the former S.S. man who had stood guard at the shower room door in the processing centre at Ravensbruck. He was the first of our actual jailers that I had seen since that time. And suddenly it was all there-the roomful of mocking men, the heaps of clothing, Betsie's pain blanched face.

He came up to me as the church was emptying, beaming and bowing. "How grateful I am for your message, Fraulein," he said. "To think that, as you say, 'He has washed my sins away'!"

His hand was thrust out to shake mine. And I, who had preached so often to the people in Bloemendaal on the need to forgive, kept my hand at my side. Even as the angry, vengeful thoughts boiled through me, I saw the sin of them. Jesus Christ had died for this man; was I going to ask for more? Lord Jesus, I prayed, forgive me and help me to forgive him.

I tried to smile; I struggled to raise my hand. I could not. I felt nothing, not the slightest spark of warmth or charity. And so again, I breathed a silent prayer. Jesus, I cannot forgive him. Give him your forgiveness. As I took his hand, the most incredible thing happened. From my shoulder along my arm and through my hand a current seemed to pass from me to him, while into my heart sprang a love for this stranger that almost overwhelmed me.

And so I discovered that it is not on our forgiveness, any more than on our goodness that the world's healing hinges, but on His. When He tells us to love our enemies, He gives, along with the command, the love itself."
Corrie Ten Boon, *The Hiding Place*

"Are you interested in reading a true-to-life life story about how I forgave my father and set myself free from the misery and angst that have plagued me for as long as I can remember? When I received a call that my estranged *father laid dying in the North of England, I acted on an impulse; an urgent need to see him engulfed me and I fled to his bedside without a second thought. I hadn't seen him for twenty-one years due to his appalling temper and a severe problem with alcohol. You may wonder why I went to see him and why I made such a rash decision? Instinct I guess. But I had absolutely no time to lose pondering on it and getting to his bedside was all that mattered to me.*

I now know that it was the best decision that I have ever made. At the time, I didn't care what he did or didn't do: I just needed to see him so I could escape from my self-imposed prison of deeply embedded anger. I needed to see my father for me and me alone. I knew deep down that something felt wrong in my life but I just couldn't quite put my finger on it; I knew that I wasn't happy but where was the elusive happiness that I was craving? I always seemed to be watching others experience joy but it was always passing me by. I always felt hollow somehow.

Six months on from meeting and forgiving my dying father, I can truly say I am a complete human being. I am happy now - no longer searching aimlessly for contentment - I have it right here in my heart, and you can too. This feeling could have been mine all along if I had just entertained the concept of forgiveness many years ago but I decided to hold on to the anger, the hurt, and the pain like a fool. And how I suffered! I have written a book about my experience and it is now available on-line. If you are interested in purchasing a copy, please send me an e-mail - I would love to hear from you. My e-mail address is: RachelFlowers38@aol.com.

If everyone forgave each other, the world could be like Heaven – think about that for a minute - we could live in a perfect world if we all uproot hatred from our hearts and sow seeds of love. Let's all heal together and make the world a better place!"
Rachel Flowers

We actually believe that by not forgiving we hold a power over that individual. Now you can begin to realize by choosing not to forgive, we actually get stuck and rot away unknowingly. It was never the other way round. It is never the individual who holds the power over you but those negative unhelpful, mind-spinning thoughts that hold you captive. You hold yourself captive. These are the thoughts you created through your perception of the situation. This perception, which has made you a prisoner, can also set the real you free, for it is you that holds the key to your own prison.

Peace of Mind Now, Not Later…

"Remember you are always in the right place at the right time!"

In order to experience peace of mind and joy in the present moment, trust and have faith that you are always in the right place at the right time. The following short story highlights this point and is taken from Lilly Walter's book, 'One Hand Typing and Keyboarding Manual: With Personal Motivational Messages from Others Who Have Overcome.'

"One of my joys and passions is my voice. I love to perform in our local community theatres. My throat became very sore during a particularly gruelling show run. It was my first time performing an operatic piece, and I was terrified that I had actually done some damage to my vocal cords. I was a lead and we were about to open. So I made an appointment with my family doctor, where I waited for an hour. I finally left in a huff, went back to work, grabbed a phone book and found a throat specialist close by. Once more, I made an appointment, and off I went.

The nurse showed me in and I sat down to wait for the doctor. I was feeling very disgruntled. I rarely get sick, and here I was, sick when I needed to be healthy. Besides, I had to take time out of my workday to go to two different doctors, both of whom kept me waiting. It was very frustrating. Why do these things have to happen? A moment later the nurse came back in, and said, "May I ask you something personal?" This seemed odd; what else do they ask you but personal questions in a doctor's office? But I looked at the nurse and replied, "Yes, of course."

"I noticed your hand," she said hesitantly.

I lost half of my left hand in a forklift accident when I was 11. I think it is one of the reasons I didn't follow my dream of performing in theatre, although everyone says, "Gee, I never noticed! You are so natural." In the back of my mind I thought that they only wanted to see perfect people on stage. No one would want to see me. But I love musical comedies, and I do have a good voice. So one day, I tried out at our local community theatre. I was the first one they cast! That was three years ago. Since then, I have been cast in almost everything I tried out for.

The nurse continued, "What I need to know is how has this affected your life." Never in the 25 years since it happened has someone asked me this. Maybe they'll say, "Does it bother you?" but never anything as sweeping as, "How has it affected your life?"

After an awkward pause, she said, "You see, I just had a baby, and her hand is like yours. I, well, need to know how it has affected your life."

"How has it affected my life?" I thought about it a bit, so I could think of the right words to say. Finally, I said, "It has affected my life, but not in a bad way. I do many things that people with two normal hands find difficult. I type about 75 words a minute, I play the guitar, I have ridden and shown horses for years, and I even have a Housemasters Degree. I'm involved in musical theatre, and I am a professional speaker. I am constantly in front of a crowd. I do television shows four or five times a year. I think it was never "difficult" because of the love and encouragement of my family. They always talked about all the great notoriety I would get because I would learn how to do things with one hand that most people had trouble doing with two. We were all very excited about that. That was the main focus, not the handicap.

"Your daughter does not have a problem. She is normal. You are the one who will teach her to think of herself as anything else. She will come to know she is "different," but you will teach her that different is wonderful. Normal means you are average. What's fun about that?"

She was silent for a while. Then she simply said, "Thank you" and walked out.

I sat there thinking, "Why do these things have to happen?" Everything happens for reasons, even that forklift falling on my hand. All the circumstances leading up to being at this doctor's office, and this moment in time happened for a reason.

The doctor came in, looked at my throat and said he wanted to anesthetize and put a probe down it to examine it. Well, singers are very paranoid about putting medical instruments down their throats, especially ones so rough they need to be anesthetized!

I said, "No thanks," and walked out.

The next day, my throat was completely better."
Lilly Walters, *One Hand Typing and Keyboarding Manual*

Serving Yourself and Others, Doing Best Actions ...

"We all have so many possible occasions for loving and yet there is so little demonstrated love in the world. People are dying alone, crying alone. Children are being abused and elderly people are spending their final days without tenderness and love. In a world where there is such an obvious need for demonstrated love, it is well to realize the enormous power we do have to help and heal people in our lives with nothing more complicated than an outstretched hand or a warm hug. Day's end is a good time to reflect on what you have done to make the world a better, more caring and loving place. If nothing springs to mind night after night, this can also be an excellent time to consider how you can change the world for the better. You need not perform monumental acts, but act on the simple things which are easily accomplished: the phone call you have not made, the note you have put off writing, the kindness you have failed to acknowledge. When it comes to giving love, the opportunities are unlimited and we are all gifted."
Leo Buscaglia, *Born For Love*

One At a Time

"A friend of ours was walking down a deserted Mexican beach at sunset. As he walked along, he began to see another man in the distance. As he

grew nearer, he noticed that the local native kept leaning down, picking something up and throwing it out into the water. Time and again, he kept hurling things out into the ocean. As our friend approached even closer, he noticed that the man was picking up starfish that had been washed up on the beach and, one at a time, he was throwing them back into the water. Our friend was puzzled. He approached the man and said "Good evening, friend. I was wondering what you are doing."

"I'm throwing these starfish back into the ocean. You see, it's low tide right now and all of these starfish have been washed up onto the shore. If I don't throw them back into the sea, they'll die up here from lack of oxygen."

"I understand," my friend replied, "but there must be thousands of starfish on this beach. You can't possibly get to all of them. There are simply too many. And don't you realize this is probably happening on hundreds of beaches all up and down this coast? Can't you see that you can't possibly make a difference?" The local native smiled, bent down and pick up yet another starfish, and as he threw it back into the sea, he replied, "Made a difference to that one!"

Chicken Soup for the Soul

Opportunities Will Find You Only If...

"Many people sit around waiting for the world to discover them, and that rarely happens. If you move toward your goals, expressing all your power, opportunity will find you as a result of your actions. For by riding your energy, knowing and believing your higher self is with you, you will be in the right place, at the right time. But make the first move, taking constant care to purify and review your life; move from negative habits into the fortress of light. Discipline is the horse you ride."

Stuart Wilde

CHAPTER 17

MORE ACTIONS TO BRING YOU BACK TO YOURSELF QUICKLY…

One of the most important things I realized so clearly after my near fatal car accident, came back to me when I was watching the movie 'Griffin & Phoenix'. **You never really know when you will do something for the last time.**

So, make sure you pay good attention to your moments and be in them fully. You will never get back the time you held your baby for the first time, or played your last game with your best childhood friend, or kissed your first love… and all those other magic moments you will never get back. So pay attention always - those moments are the juice of life and unknowingly could be your last time!

Observe the voices in your head that frequently take you away.

Pay clear focused attention to those repetitive thoughts, especially those old voices and movies that do not help you - you know the ones that have been playing for many years making your life worse rather than better. Instead watch yourself, "the thinker", like you would listen to someone else and observe without blame, judgment or analysis. This will definitely take the charge, fear, frustration or worrying feeling out of those thoughts. This really works and most definitely kills dead most of your problems. It is the feelings of frustration, anxiety or fear, attached to those thoughts that are the issue, not the thoughts themselves. Take that away and you will get greater clarity. It will also give you the sense of your own real presence. It will feel even more amazingly the more you do it, guaranteed. One day you will find yourself smiling or laughing at those voices in your head! Now that is a day to celebrate!

- **Watch your defensiveness - any kind of defensiveness within yourself!**

What exactly are you defending? Perhaps an illusionary identity or image in your mind, probably purely ego driven. Again, as before be a witness and observer of your own mind without judgment, blame or analysis. Those patterns of thoughts and the behaviours linked to them will then quickly dissolve. It will end all anxious, frustrating, power games, including arguments. A little self-observation can end all that pain and constant suffering.

And you know how this destroys any kind of relationship. Enough said, your choice.

Remember clearly that power over others is a major weakness disguised as strength. You know true power is within and only becomes available to you without blame, judgment or analysis. Do it and see everything around you unfold. Words alone will not give you the absolution you want or seek, just do it, see and feel it.

Meditate everyday in the simple ways I have mentioned. Draw your consciousness away from your mind activities. Create gaps of "no-mind" in which you are highly switched on but not thinking! This is truly the essence of genuine meditation.

- **Remember: All problems are just illusions of the mind! And they are definitely part of life and solvable. Remember that there is no need for them to feel so heavy, that would be one's mind playing with us to think it that way… catch it early, and do not let it completely engulf you!**

"Forget about your life situation for a while and pay attention to your life.

Your life situation exists in time. Your life is now.

Your life situation is mind-stuff. Your life is real.

Find the "narrow gate that leads to life". It is called the now. Narrow your life down to this moment. Your life situation may be full of problems – most life situations are – but find out if you have any problem at this moment. Not tomorrow or in ten minutes, but now. Do you have a problem now?"
Eckhart Tolle

This will help you to observe your mind before it takes you on a nightmare trip! If you answered the question with a yes – then you have a problem so ask yourself some of the questions we've already discussed, like 'What must I do to make it better from now? What else do I feel I must do?' Keep asking and keep listing…

- **Always use your senses fully wherever you are now…**

Which means do not interpret or make commentaries like a radio show announcer or you will miss it all. Listen to sounds without judgments… Listen to the silence underneath or between the sounds while breathing… Touch someone or anything and feel it…be there with its being without judgments or interpreting, nor comments…

- **Keep observing the rhythm of your breathing…**

Feel the airflow in and out, feel the energy in your body again with neither interpretations nor judgments.

Be the change you want to see and feel in the world. Begin today! All it takes is a conscious deep breath.

- **Do you have joy in your life now or on whatever you are doing?**

Is there joy, ease and lightness in what you are doing? If not, you are not living in the moment. It does not mean that you need to change what you are doing; it may be just enough to change how you do it. Remember that how you do it is always more important than "what" you do. Give your best to the doing rather than the result. All that may be needed is an attitude adjustment.

"Give your fullest attention to whatever the moment presents. This implies that you also completely accept what is, because you cannot give your full attention to something and at the same time resist it."
Eckhart Tolle

As soon as you give any moment 'all of you', your unhappiness and struggles will dissolve like a hard sugar cube in warm water. Your life will genuinely flow and will grow with joy, while being at ease.

- **Melt down the mind games!**

"On the level of your thinking, you will find a great deal of resistance in the form of judgment, discontent, and mental projection away from the Now. On the emotional level, there will be an undercurrent of unease, tension, boredom, or nervousness. Both are aspects of the mind in its habitual resistance mode"
Eckhart Tolle

Be very interested in and focused on what goes on inside you, rather than what is outside. Remember that if you get the inside right, the outside will follow.

Ask yourself: "Am I genuinely at ease at this very moment?" or "What do I genuinely feel is going on inside me at this very moment?"

Then ask, "What must I now do to feel at ease? Or what must I do to just feel better towards being at ease?" or simply "What must I do right now to genuinely feel better? What must happen for me to just feel much better?"

Then do it immediately without judgment, blame or analysis.

Ok, let's look even deeper and more boldly... What kind of thoughts is your mind giving you now?

- **What do you feel now?**

Observe it through your body first, is there tension? How are you breathing? Are you at ease? Once you catch yourself being lost, unsure and feeling unease, then ask: **'what am I avoiding, if I am honest with myself? What am I resisting right now with myself? What am I denying?' If your mind says I don't know then say to yourself 'I know I do not know, and that's ok, but if I did know what do I feel it is?'** Remember that with constant practice, your power of observation and resolve will get easier and you will get stronger at being your own advisor. You will remember that you are your own personal expert, without the ego strapped on! (Meaning again without judgment, blame and analysis).

- **Are you often stressed?**

Not "being here now" but wanting to be "there instead" causes stress. Remember that too many minds, is no mind at all. It also makes you feel like you are all over the place. When you find yourself planning ahead or fantasizing about the past, simply bring yourself back to the present, such as literally calling your spirit back, say it aloud if necessary! Then be fully present in the moment to whatever is in front of you or at hand.

Ask yourself: 'Are you creating guilt, self pity, resentment, anger, regret or pride with your thinking approach?' If this is so, you are creating a false sense of self. Let go of these deep unhelpful feelings, forgive and move on so that you can celebrate your life presently. Only refer to your past when it is absolutely relevant to the moment.

- **Do you wait for life to happen to you and make up valid reasons?**

How much of your life do you spend waiting? I am not talking about waiting in a queue at the bank or in a traffic jam… I am talking about waiting for your children to grow up before you do anything or waiting for your next holiday or waiting for a loving relationship to present itself to you or waiting for success or to make money or be important.

Remember that most people spend their entire life waiting to genuinely start living. Living now completely eludes their world cocooned in their minds with huge limits. This makes waiting only a state of mind. Now how does that bring joy into your life exactly? Waiting means you really do not want to be here, you have an inner conflict between here and now and your fantasy projected future where you really want to be. Your quality of life is greatly reduced as you lose the present. If you feel something is missing or a lack of some kind, you will continue to feel unfulfilled no matter what you do.

So, ask yourself 'What else must you do to create or bring more living, and joy into your life now with whatever you have?'

What type of attitude do you live by? Is the glass half full or half empty? Are you grateful for your existence, for the breath that you breathe? Your money will buy you many distractions but they will come and go, and in the long run, every distraction will still leave you feeling empty. The hole will never be filled until you live in the now, when you learn to observe rather than judge etc. If you see and feel joy, abundance and love then you will attract more of it into your life.

As a warm up... next time when someone says to you "I am so sorry for keeping you waiting… you can reply, no problem. I was not waiting. I was here enjoying myself (in joy with myself)."
Eckhart Tolle

Please never be a fugitive to your self, or worse your own soul, waiting for the future.

- **The past will never survive if you are here, now**!

" Whatever you need to know about the unconscious past in you, the challenges of the present will bring it out. If you delve into the past, it will become a bottomless pit: There is always more. You may think that you need more time to understand the past or become free of it, in other words, that the future will eventually free you of the past. This is a delusion. Only the present can free you of the past. More time cannot free you of time."
Eckhart Tolle

Again, know that the more energy and time you give to the past, the more you will give it more charge and life. You will never find yourself by staying in the past. You will find the genuine you by coming into the present… the only living light there is.

- **Find the crystals that close your gaps and that energize you too…**

Certain things do not make thinking sense. There are many mysteries on the earth that we do not yet understand. Things that are incredible. All you have to do is look up at the stars at night and see the vastness, the stillness, the beauty, and the wonder. Experience your connection with nature as it fills the human spirit with a sense of peace and love.

Crystals also give a sense of peace, clarity and being grounded. They have powerful healing attributes such as clearing out chakras. There are many different types of crystals and you can test them out by wearing them or placing them one by one on the different chakras of your body. Moldavite, black onyx, rose quartz, malachite, tiger-eye, turquoise, emerald and citrine are a few of my favourites.

The chrysopras is my stone for everyday use; it aids the healing of pain and balances out grief and negativity. This crystal helps me with my work and healing with clients. The Moldavite is probably my favourite as it is a crystal that shifts aside all limits and takes you back to the source. It is not for everyone as its effects can be very strong.

"This celestial gem bridges Heaven and Earth - not everyone can handle the effect! It acts as a catalyst to awaken and accelerate you're spiritual growth. It is a high frequency stone that opens up your vision; you see the bigger picture, the cosmic reality, and a transpersonal view from a universal level. Through this doorway to higher states of consciousness Moldavite pulls you into a place of illumination and assention towards unity and oneness- the source. Moldavite shows us that there no limits to what you can achieve." Anonymous

Find the crystals that feel right for you in your moments. Wear them and feel them for a while, get good advice from gifted guides, and check out how you feel about it. The time may come when you do not need a particular stone anymore, do not just stay with it because of your past wonderful memories or experiences. You will know when it is time to let it go or it may decide to leave you when it has served its purpose.

- **Make sure you die, before you die!**

Ignoring "what is" is just self-suicide without the chance to choose your true path, and your authentic gifts will never truly be realised. When we ignore what is, it will resurface over and over again, making one edgy and reactive. Remember to be a focused observer and witness to yourself constantly. Your mind wants to be alive and take over; it is always hungry for more spin, until we decide to acknowledge what is happening and to make a better choice. Sometimes, we just have to say no, not today!

CHAPTER 18

CHOOSE GENUINE OR FALSE BEING. THE PRICE...

Remembering to have self-truth, and to follow it through, means consciousness.

Without this, you simply have no choice. Choice really begins in the moment you decide to cut off or divorce yourself from your mind. This can only be achieved when you choose to be in the moment, never later, as this is only the mind fooling you again.

Until you are living in the moment, you will be unconscious, asleep, and unaware no matter how book smart or well read you are. You are forced to think, feel, act, and talk in a certain way, mostly through the conditioning of the pictures, movies, and sounds that have always been running, unchecked or updated.

Let me summarise some core principles that I have come to understand from my own journey. If you are someone, like most of us, who has issues with their parents, if you hold onto even mild resentment about something they did or did not do, then

your belief is that they had a choice - but this is truly a mind led illusion.

How come you ask? It means you are in your mind. Your mind is taking a trip without you on board, with all your pain, confusion and suffering!

We have all been on a trip to nowhere with all of our baggage. The only thing left to do is to forgive, have compassion, and have empathy for others and ourselves. Forgiving yourself, and others is truly the beginning of being in the now and feeling alive. The only way you will access yourself and get your genuine power of choice is to be here now. So engage, create and get to know better habits that heal you daily.

In doing this, you will make your unhelpful past simply powerless over you. You will then realise, from the heart that "no thing" you ever did or felt can really come close to the bright essence of who you genuinely are. Then the past will truly be done, and then you will be free and light in mind and spirit!

I wish you genuine joy in your awakened self, including all the gifts, and surprises that await you. As I always say to my close friends and family, 'Genuinely stay light in mind and in your heart and then do it all from there…'

Let me finish with a poem that helped me when things got very tough. Nelson Mandela also loves this poem and it helped him during his most difficult times in prison.

Invictus *(meaning: unconquered, unconquerable, undefeated…)*

"Out of the night that covers me,
Black as the Pit from pole to pole,
I thank whatever gods may be
For my unconquerable soul.

In the fell clutch of circumstance
I have not winced nor cried aloud.
Under the bludgeonings of chance
My head is bloody, but unbowed.

Beyond this place of wrath and tears
Looms but the Horror of the shade,
And yet the menace of the years
Finds, and shall find, me unafraid.

It matters not how strait the gate,
How charged with punishments the scroll.
I am the master of my fate:
I am the captain of my soul."
William Ernest Henley

Printed in Great Britain
by Amazon